Jenny Thomas and Diane White

Australia • Brazil • Japan • Korea • Mexico • Singapore • Spain • United Kingdom • United States

Achievement English @ Year 11
1st Edition
Jenny Thomas
Diane White

Typesetter: Book Design Ltd
Production controller: Siew Han Ong
Reprint: Natalie Orr

Any URLs contained in this publication were checked for currency during the production process. Note, however, that the publisher cannot vouch for the ongoing currency of URLs.

Revised edition of ISBN 9780170189477.

Acknowledgements
Our grateful thanks to all past and present colleagues who have so generously shard their expertise, creativity and resources. English departments thrive on you collegiality.
The authors and publisher wish to thank the following people and organisations for permission to use the resources in this textbook. Every effort has been made to trace and acknowledge all copyright owners of material used in this book. In most cases this was successful and copyright is acknowledged as requested. However, if any infringement has occurred the publishers tender their apologies and invite the copyright holders to contact them.
Page 6, Under the Mountain courtesy of Maurice Gee; page 7, A Windy Day courtesy of Andrew Young; pages 8-9, advertisements courtesy of Kiwibank; page 15, The Modern Girl's Guide to ... Swimming Togs courtesy of NZ Women's Weekly and Sarah-Kate Lynch; page 17, Fewer Children go to school on foot - study, 2008, courtesy of Giles Brown, Fairfax New Zealand Limited; page 18, A mountain of stupidity 2008, courtesy, of Fairfax New Zealand Limited; page 20, Love and Other excuses courtesy of Jane Westaway; page 26, Greasies to go ... courtesy of The New Zealand Herald; page 29, Routeburn courtesy of Mike White and North & South/ACP Media Ltd; page 34, So Gay courtesy of Steve Braunias and Sunday Star Times, image courtesy of Getty Images; page 37, Extract from The God of Small Things by Arundhati Roy published by HarperCollins Publishers, London, 1997. Reprinted by permission of HarperCollins Publishers Ltd. © ; page 41, Wintery Gloom, courtesy of David Montgomery (Tommy Gorden); page 43, Preludes courtesy of T.S Eliot and Faber and Faber Ltdl page 45, Pet Shop courtesy of Louis MacNeice and David Hingham Associates; page 47, Grief on the Whanganui River courtesy of Anne McDonnell; page 49, Being Sixteen courtesy of Michael Khan; page 51, Kite courtesy of Anne French; page 53-54, The Lady of Shalott courtesy of Alfred Lord Tennyson; page 57, painting by William Holden Hunt courtesy of Manchester Art Gallery Picture Library; page 60, advertisement courtesy of Land Transport Authority; page 63, advertisement courtesy of The Auckland Museum; page 65, advertisement courtesy of GlaxoSmithKline; page 68, advertisement courtesy of DairyNZ; page 72, Why Don't Your Talk To Me? courtesy of Alistair Campbell; page 73, Compulsion courtesy of Tania Kelly Roxborogh; page 75, Mana Wahine courtesy of Terri Hudson; page 72, Thistles courtesy of Faber and Faber; page 81, Cook's Sites. Revisiting History courtesy of Otago University Press; page 83, The Mess We Made at Port Chalmers, courtesy of Cilla McQueen and Otago University Press; page 84, extract courtesy of Forest and Bird; page 89, A Kestrel for a Knave, Hodder Graphic, courtesy of Hodder Murray; Page 90, Travels with my Mother, courtesy of Peter Calder; page 110, The Soldier courtesy of Rupert Brooke; page 111, Dulce et Decorum est courtesy of Willfred Owen; page 143, Is Santa Real? courtesy of Bryce Caird.

National Library of New Zealand Cataloguing-in-Publication Data
Thomas, Jenny.
Achievement English @ year 11 / Jenny Thomas and Diane White.
3rd ed.
Previous ed.: 2008.
ISBN 978-0-17-024422-0
1. English language—Rhetoric. 2. English language—Composition and exercises. I. White, Diana. II. Title.
808.042—dc 22

Cengage Learning Australia
Level 7, 80 Dorcas Street
South Melbourne, Victoria Australia 3205

Cengage Learning New Zealand
Unit 4B Rosedale Office Park
331 Rosedale Road, Albany, North Shore 0632, NZ

For learning solutions, visit **cengage.com.au**

Printed in China by China Translation & Printing Services.
4 5 6 7 8 9 21 20 19 18 17

Contents

When you see this icon refer to Chapter 11 for a detailed list of the terminology used in relation to that text type.

Year 11.

You've made it to the first Level!

YEAR 11 IS A REALLY IMPORTANT YEAR.

You have graduated from the junior school to the senior school.

Year 11 is probably the year when you will tackle external assessment for the first time. You've been working towards this throughout Year 9 and Year 10 and you will have absorbed many of the essential skills you need to succeed at **NCEA Level 1.**

Think about what your work was like at the beginning of Year 9. You'll see that you've already learnt a lot!

Achievement English @ Year 11 is designed as a workbook for you personally to use to support your study of English this year. It will:

- help you hone your skills
- give you lots of useful practice
- give you plenty of good advice about how to achieve in English this year.

All of the examples and exercises have been chosen with you in mind and with reference to the kinds of assessments you will find in both external and internal Standards.

We are confident that you are ready to begin,

so let's get going . . .

ISBN 9780170244220

Check it!

What does all this really mean?

Close Read
Reading for meaning
Comprehension
Understand
Unfamiliar Text
Enlarge
Precise
Interpret
Analyse

A key skill in the study of English is to understand and analyse text, and as you already know, a text might be a novel, a short story, a magazine article, a poem, a poster, a still from a film, a business card etc. The skill of close reading applies to *everything* that you read, view or hear. And it is going to be increasingly important to be able to show your understanding of significant aspects of visual, oral and written text as you progress through senior school. This is not a skill that can be taught in isolation.

While it is true that your assessments will separate the close reading of unfamiliar written text (AS 1.3) and visual and oral text (AS 1.11), if you think about it you are actually using these skills in virtually all aspects of your English course, and in actual fact much of the assessment in your other subjects too!

This part of the book is designed to support the close reading instruction and practice in your classroom with your teacher. It is not just a way to answer particular assessments.

In *Achievement English @ Year 11* we have chosen to present the methods for close reading in one section. So don't be surprised when you find a section on visual text in this section … remember when you work with Achievement English you are learning skills, not just practising assessment.

ISBN 9780170244220

Before we go forward, let's go back

Let's make sure that you have some of the essential terminology that you will need this year. We will be focusing on Close Reading, but you will use your knowledge of the terminology for English study in all aspects of your course this year.

We are going to begin by giving you three texts to look at, so that you can check where you are up to in your knowledge of terminology.

Things to do with prose ...

This year you will be expected to analyse different types of prose: fiction, non-fiction, extracts from novels, short stories, magazines, newspapers etc.

This extract, from Maurice Gee's novel *Under the Mountain,* is describing a warm, protective light around three-year-old twins lost in the bush. People are searching for them.

Read it carefully and then complete the task on the next page.

Indefinite article

A light like a flame was moving in the trees, so bright it made them hide their eyes. It floated high above the ground, turning like a mist through the trunks.

'What is it?' They ran over the clearing, but as they ran it vanished, and they stood bewildered in the weak glow of their torches. In that same instant, deep back in the bush, the light came down beside Rachel and Theo Matheson. It covered them like a blanket, flowed round and under them, soft and honey-coloured, drew down and dulled itself. Warmth flowed into the limbs of the sleeping children. They smiled and murmured. All night they slept as though in their beds at home. They dreamed happy dreams. The light lay still and warm over them, murmuring like a hive of bees.

Greyness came through the black night of the bush. Trucks and cars roared into the Matheson farm. Policemen, farmers, gathered for a second day of the search. Dogs barked. A helicopter chattered down the valley from the town.

ISBN 9780170244220

We want to use this short passage for 'the naming of parts'. When you have read the passage, use the list below and find as many of the elements as you can. Highlight and annotate each term.

We have done the first one for you.

LANGUAGE LIST

Parts of Speech

- [x] Indefinite article
- [ ] Definite article
- [ ] Verb
- [ ] Preposition
- [ ] Pronoun
- [ ] Possessive adjective
- [ ] Common noun
- [ ] Proper noun
- [ ] Adjective
- [ ] Conjunction

Syntax

- [ ] Simple sentence
- [ ] Compound sentence
- [ ] Compound-complex sentence

Figures of Speech

- [ ] Simile
- [ ] Alliteration
- [ ] Repetition
- [ ] Personification
- [ ] Onomatopoeia

Things to do with poetry ...

You will also be expected to read and understand poems. Sometimes students believe that this will be difficult. Remember, poems are simply the best words in the best order.

Read this poem carefully and then complete the task on the next page.

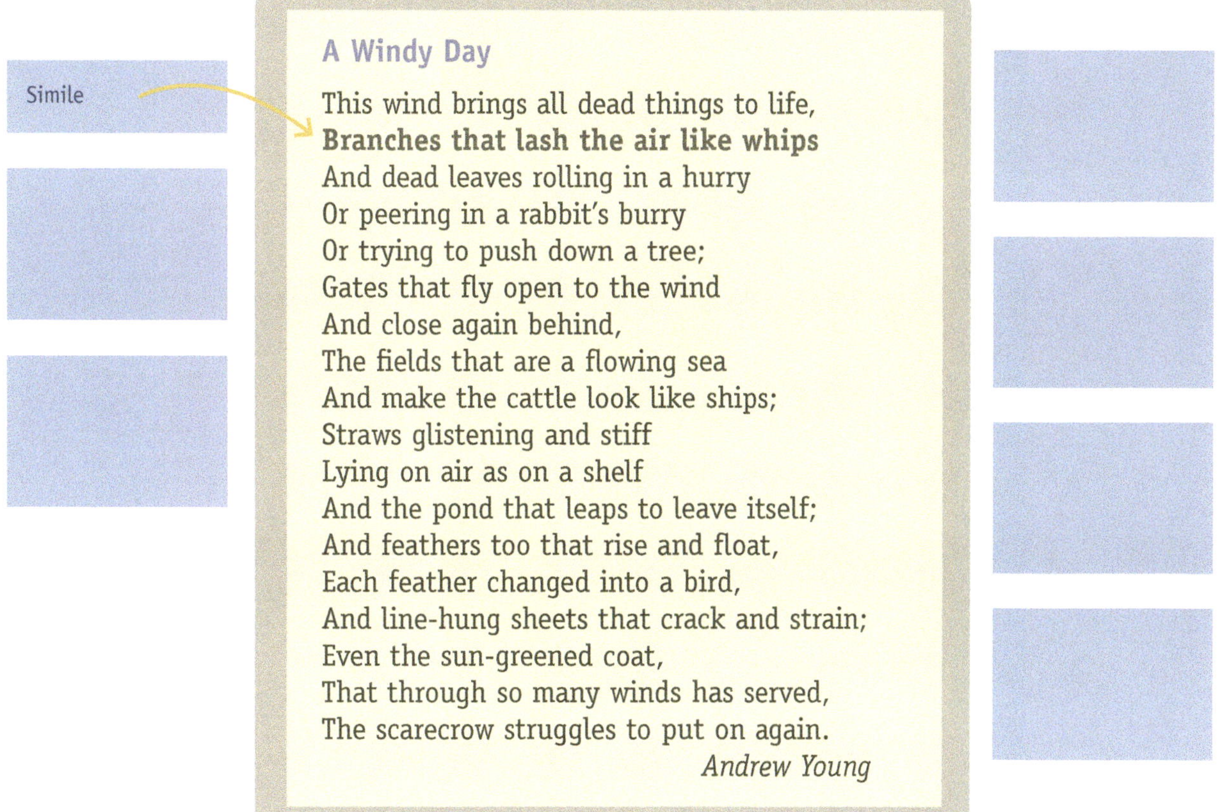

A Windy Day

This wind brings all dead things to life,
Branches that lash the air like whips
And dead leaves rolling in a hurry
Or peering in a rabbit's burry
Or trying to push down a tree;
Gates that fly open to the wind
And close again behind,
The fields that are a flowing sea
And make the cattle look like ships;
Straws glistening and stiff
Lying on air as on a shelf
And the pond that leaps to leave itself;
And feathers too that rise and float,
Each feather changed into a bird,
And line-hung sheets that crack and strain;
Even the sun-greened coat,
That through so many winds has served,
The scarecrow struggles to put on again.

Andrew Young

ISBN 9780170244220

Find, highlight and annotate as many examples of the following as you can:

Parts of Speech

- [x] Simile
- [ ] Metaphor
- [ ] Personification
- [ ] Alliteration
- [ ] Onomatopoeia
- [ ] Repeated structure
- [ ] Rhyme

LANGUAGE LIST

Bonus Point:
Can you remember why an author would use a semicolon?

When you have looked carefully at the poem and you have seen how many figures of speech the poet has included, you will appreciate that he has illustrated beautifully what happens on a windy day. You might draw a picture from these words.

Things to do with visuals ...

The third type of text you may be asked to analyse is called visual text. This may be an advertisement, a poster, a book cover etc.

Visuals have an additional set of techniques which you need to be aware of – techniques to do with layout and colour, balance, contrast, symbols etc.

Read this visual text carefully and then complete the task on the next page.

kiwibank It's ours

Being a student, chances are you've got hardly any spare cash. So every buck you can save on your banking counts. It's money you're better off spending on little things here and there, to make your shoestring life as a student slightly more bearable. That's why Kiwibank offers students better value student banking with no annual account or transaction fees, free ATM withdrawals at all banks' ATMs on university campuses and an additional fee-free flat account.

Plus there's plenty more reasons to sign up – check them out at **www.kiwibank.co.nz/tertiarypack**

To be eligible for the Tertiary Pack, you must be studying full or part time at a New Zealand University, Polytech or an NZQA approved institution for a minimum of one year. Service fees may apply. Kiwibank's Disclosure Statement is available from any local Kiwibank or www.kiwibank.co.nz. Kiwibank Limited's terms and conditions and lending criteria apply.

ISBN 9780170244220

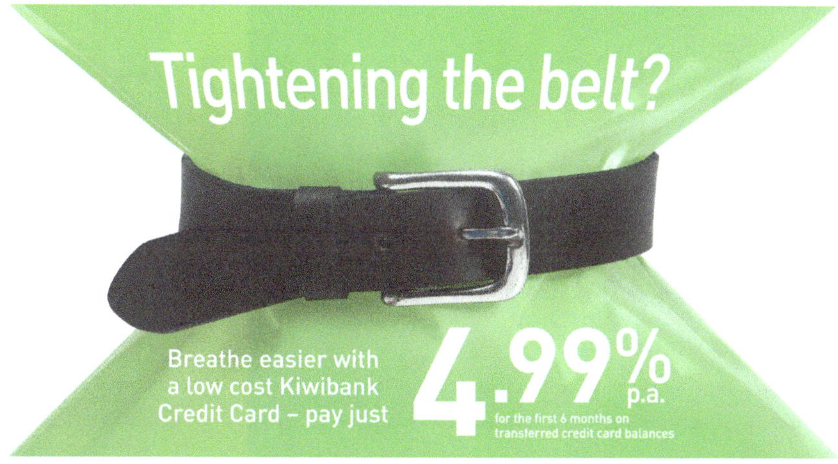

Using both these advertisements, find, highlight and annotate these techniques:

LANGUAGE LIST

○ Pun	○ Dash	○ Cliché
○ Logo	○ Adjectives	○ Rule of thirds
○ Slogan	○ Rhetorical question	○ Symbol
○ Personal pronouns	○ Dominant Visual Feature	○ Contrast
○ Compound word	○ Contractions	○ Headline
○ Comparative	○ Repetition	○ Body copy
○ Colloquial language	○ Imperative	○ Font (choice/ changes in)
○ Alliteration		

Same product. Different audiences. How can you tell?

____

____

____

____

How did you go?

We have just asked you to find 45 features of language. Look back over your work. How many did you find?

- If you found 40 or more, you're ready to move on.
- If you found 30-39, use the language list at the back of this book to remind yourself of what you have forgotten.
- If you found fewer than 30, then it might be a good idea to go back to *How to … Achieve in Year 10 English* for a refresher course!

ISBN 9780170244220

3 Close Reading – learning to read and understand Unfamiliar Text

You will have been taught how to 'close read' texts every year that you have studied English. In the earlier books of this series (*How to …* and *Building On …*) we taught you to analyse text by thinking of the types of questions asked.

1 On the surface

One of the skills that close reading tests is your ability to understand what is happening in the text. Therefore the first type of question you are likely to meet is the basic literal question where the answer is clearly written in the text.

These questions are likely to be based around *facts*. Things such as:

- Who?
- What?
- When?
- Where?
- Why?
- How?

In other words you will be looking for factual information.

2 Technical

You are going to hear the word 'style' quite often when you study English. Style means the way something has been written. To help you understand the writer's craft, you will begin by looking at his or her techniques. This will include things like vocabulary (the words selected by the writer) and structure (the way the sentences are ordered). You will be asked to identify the basic language features.

To answer a technical question successfully, you will need to have some idea about the intended audience, be able to recognise the language used and the way the text has been put together.

3 Search and think

These are implied questions. You will have to 'read between the lines' of the text to answer questions in this section. It is likely you will need to use your own knowledge and thinking, as well as information from the text, to answer these questions.

For many of you these will be the trickiest of all questions because they demand that you think carefully about what is being said and then think about what that means. You may believe this is difficult, but in fact you do it every day. You look at people's body language, tone of voice, the words they choose to use and you make a judgement about how you will respond. Search and think questions ask you to do the same thing. Read the passage and make a judgement about what is going on that is not written about. Read between the lines of the text to answer these questions.

SO TO RECAP …

- You know the terminology
- You know the types of questions asked
- You know what is required to answer them.

ISBN 9780170244220

HOWEVER ...

At this stage it is likely that you have been taught to look for information, to find techniques and perhaps to comment on the way they create a specific effect. To make progress in your understanding and analysis of text, you need to see how the text has been created as a complete piece, in a planned and deliberate way.

To help you learn to do this we need to introduce the concept of Style

You need to see how a piece has been crafted intentionally: in a certain style, with a certain purpose, for a certain audience.

Style

We are sure you will know the word style in connection with fashion. In the world of clothing, style can be formal (school uniform), flamboyant (rapper), grunge (rock band), sporty (athletic), girlie (pink and frilly) etc.

When it comes to the written word, style is *the way the author writes*, rather than what the author writes about.

For example, if four people were at a car accident, and were all asked to write down what happened, all four would probably have a different way of telling the same facts.

A policeman would probably give just the facts, in a very serious, straightforward style.

> *'The Ford Escort was travelling at approximately seventy kilometres an hour along Princes Street.'*

A reporter for a newspaper like the *New Zealand Herald* might give a much more sensational and vivid account.

> *'Black rubber stripes along a city street mark the site of a major crash.'*

The man whose car had been hit might write in a very angry and emotional style.

> *'A lunatic almost wrecked my Beamer. The idiot charged down the street stupidly ignoring the speed limit. He should be locked up and the keys thrown away.'*

The driver might be more defensive.

> *'I was driving along, not very fast, when a huge dog leapt out from a driveway. I couldn't do anything, really. It wasn't my fault.'*

TYPES OF STYLES YOU MIGHT COME ACROSS THIS YEAR INCLUDE:

Persuasive HUMOROUS Dramatic

Emotional Colloquial Formal

Be careful ... sometimes a piece of writing might use more than one style.

> Think of it as directors creating different types (genres) of films for different audiences: the chick flick, thriller, animation, drama, adventure, political, documentary, wester, sci-fi, art-house etc. Each type is aimed at a different part of the cinema-going audience.

ISBN 9780170244220

So ... how do we find the style?

The following diagram draws together all of the threads you will use to identify style. It will provide you with a useful reference chart whenever you look at a piece of unfamiliar text.

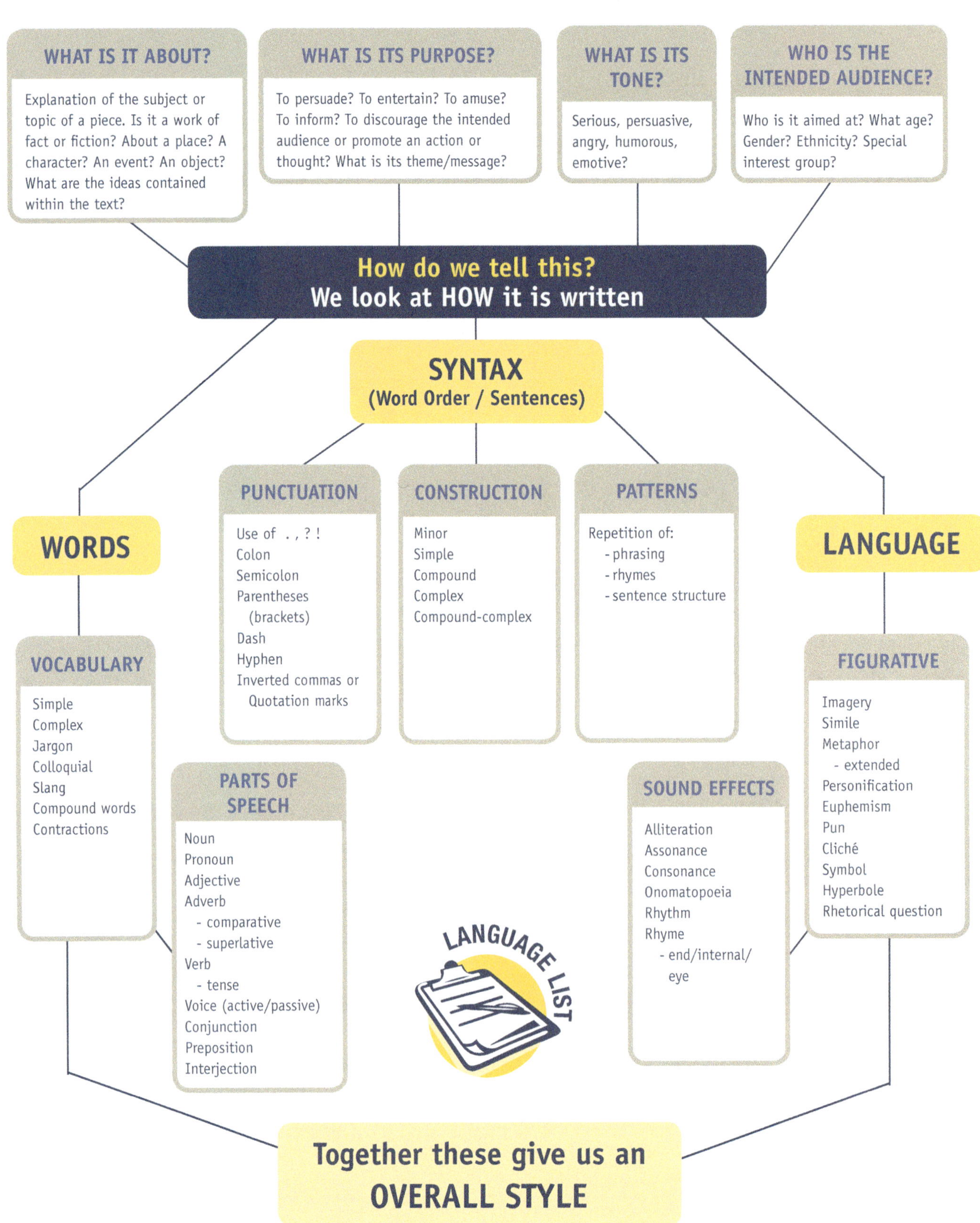

ISBN 9780170244220

Before we go any further ...

Close reading – test yourself

Fill in the gaps.

1 The beat of a poem is called ______________.

2 When a non-living thing is given living characteristics it is called ______________.

3 A comparison between two things using 'like' or 'as' is a ______________.

4 ______________ is a specialised language used by people who work together.

5 An ______________ ______________ is used at the end of a sentence to show strong feeling.

6 You find extra information inside ______________.

7 The section of the reading/viewing public at which a text is aimed is called the ______________ ______________.

8 A ______________ is a word that joins sentences.

9 Highly colloquial expressions unsuitable in general conversation are ______________.

10 A question designed to suggest rather than demand an answer is called a ______________ ______________.

11 A ______________ sentence does not contain a verb.

12 A phrase used to express a request, order or command is an ______________.

13 ______________ language is relaxed and informal language used in common conversation.

14 ______________ is the deliberate repetition of consonant sounds at the beginning of words.

15 A ______________ plays on different meanings of the same word.

16 A writer who wishes to involve the reader will frequently use ______________.

17 A ______________ is added to the end of a word to alter its meaning.

18 ______________ shows the writer's attitude to the topic.

19 ______________ is where words and/or phrases are repeated for emphasis or for special effect.

20 ______________ tell us how, when or where an action takes place.

ISBN 9780170244220

Why do professional writers choose certain techniques?

Many close reading questions ask you to not only identify language features but explain why an author has chosen to use that technique. Complete the following grid to assess your knowledge. Go back to *How to ... Achieve in Year 10 English* if you need a reminder.

Technique	*Definition*	**Why used**
Simile	A phrase that compares two things using 'like' or 'as'.	
Personification	When a non-living thing is given living characteristics.	
Adverb	Tells us how, when or where an action takes place.	
Minor sentence	A sentence without a completed verb.	
Onomatopoeia	When the sound of the word imitates or suggests the meaning or noise of the action.	
Repetition	Where words or phrases are repeated.	
Pun	An expression that plays on different meanings of the same word.	
Rhetorical question	A question that does not require an answer.	
Assonance	The deliberate repetition of the same vowel sound followed by a different consonant sound.	
Alliteration	The repetition of consonant sounds, usually at the beginning of words.	
Pronoun	A pronoun may be used instead of a noun.	
Colloquial language	Relaxed and informal language that is used in common conversation.	
Metaphor	A phrase in which one thing is identified with another.	
Adjective	A describing word.	

ISBN 9780170244220

Don't panic! Let's show you what we mean

Here is a column from the *New Zealand Woman's Weekly* that has a distinctive style. Read it carefully and answer the questions that follow.

The modern girl's guide to... Swimming togs

FBI ILLUSTRATOR: HELEN CASEY

● At the risk of sounding like a wet blanket, I wish the nicer weather would go away.

It's just I'm lying awake, night after night, worried sick about global warming, the Greenhouse effect and having to buy new togs.

There's something horribly wrong with a world in which the time you need to buy something which covers less of you than anything else coincides with the time when most of you should be kept covered up.

As it is, the first foray – usually about now – into your local tog emporium often ends in severe trauma, resulting from a pale, pudgy woman who looks a bit like you, only sadder, staring out of a mirror. It makes you realise how good you are at hiding stuff.

Of course, it doesn't help that the changing room lights play tricks with your cellulite and those sensible knickers, left on in the interests of hygiene, can hardly be said to add to your allure – like you need more lumps!

As for the helpful assistant who opens the door to see how you are getting on – well, she deserves to be in therapy for the rest of her life. Doesn't she know there are two occasions when a girl must be left in complete and utter isolation? (The other involves chocolate.)

Once, I had a bikini. I think I was seven. I remember it vividly, because the pants were made of towelling and had a porous lining, which meant large amounts of sand became trapped between the layers and gave a pronounced sag.

Now, I have that sag all on my own.

At some stage in my teens, there was a two-piece which involved bikini pants and a short halter-neck dress which covered several regions. This was quite popular – but it disintegrated after about 14 years.

More recently it's become a full-time job traipsing the stores, looking for vertical stripes and rouching in the right places.

This year, though, I got smart.

We're talking mail order. Why risk exposing bits of yourself – which should have been waxed off months ago – in a semi-public place when you can do so in the comfort of your own home, with the curtains closed and the lights turned off?

Having a selection of togs arrive in your mailbox takes the trauma right out of it. You have to be careful not to put the trauma right back in, though.

It helps to have a full-length mirror – poorly lit, of course. At our new flat in Wellington, we only have a bathroom mirror which, for the purposes of modelling my new swimsuit selection, I plonked on top of the laundry basket. This showed me only my thigh and stomach region.

When I came to, I tried putting the mirror on the dresser but this only showed me from the neck up. How could I tell if the floral centre-panel was doing its job?

Then, I put the mirror on the floor which showed only my ankles. I liked that a lot but it hardly helped.

Finally, I put the mirror back on the laundry basket and crouched down so I could see the top of my togs, then leapt up so I could see the middle and bottom.

Hmm. You know, with the right needlework and a bit of glue, I reckon there's another year left in that teenage two-piece...

1 Who is the target audience for this passage?

2 What kind of style is the writer creating in this passage?

3 This passage is written in the first person. Why?

ISBN 9780170244220

4 As this is your first passage we're going to help you out. The humorous tone/style of this article is created by using:

- amusing anecdotes
- exaggeration (hyperbole)
- alliteration
- colloquial language.

Go back to the column and, using a variety of coloured highlighters, find as many examples of the features listed above as you can.

5 Write a paragraph and, in your own words, explain why the intended audience would find this passage amusing.

ISBN 9780170244220

Let's go a step further ...

Here are two items from a newspaper. The first, from the *Christchurch Press,* is a news item, the second is an editorial from the *Taranaki Daily News.* They are both based around a University of Otago study on children walking to school.

We have highlighted and annotated some of the features that illustrate the difference between the two styles of writing.

Carefully read each piece and answer the questions that follow.

Fewer children go to school on foot – study

Giles Brown

The sight of children walking to school may become a thing of the past if current trends continue, a University of Otago study predicts.

A survey of 1500 Dunedin primary schoolchildren and their parents found car ownership, ethnicity and family wealth were all behind a decline in the numbers of children making the morning hike from breakfast table to classroom.

Of the children surveyed, about a third had walked to school.

A questionnaire sent out to parents revealed half of the children walked to school less than three times a week.

The director of the university's social and behavioural research unit, Dr Tony Reeder, said the study was "objective evidence" of a widely accepted trend.

The study found the number of children living further from school was a big factor in the decline.

Children living within 1km of their school were 30 times more likely to make the trip by foot than those living 3km away.

"The closure of neighbourhood schools is likely to have contributed to the reduction in the number of children who walk to school," Reeder said.

The modern car habit also drew families away from walking to school.

"We want everything quickly these days and we want to be right there right now," he said.

Children from lower socio-economic backgrounds or Pacific Island or Maori families were more likely to walk to school.

Children in schools of socio-economic deciles two and four were more than twice as likely to walk.

Boys were a third more likely to walk than girls, and Years 4 to 6 were over two-thirds more likely to walk than younger children.

Children whose parents had walked to school when they were young were over a third more likely to walk too.

Reeder said this did not mean a decline in those walking to school would see the habit disappear completely.

"I think it could without intervention, but those interventions are beginning to happen now."

The push play manager for Sport and Recreation New Zealand (Sparc), Deb Hurdle, said she thought the increasing cost of petrol might see families walk to school more often.

"People might start to think more seriously about whether they do take their car for those little journeys," she said.

Thorrington School in the Christchurch suburb of Cashmere has done its own study of walking habits.

"We really concentrated on those living within 1km and looked at targets about how many people we wanted walking to school," said principal Paul Armitage.

The number of children walking peaked at 78 per cent two weeks ago. "Children that come after having had fresh air and a little bit of exercise do come in more ready to learn."

Stepping out: a walking bus makes its way to a school. Photo: Fairfax

Annotations:

- 3 reasons later expanded
- Statistic
- Expert
- Another significant factor
- Statistic
- Reasons why those DO walk
- Expert says in future petrol ↑, walking ↑
- Air + exercise = ready to learn

Saturday, April 12, 2008

Editorial = opinion

A mountain of stupidity

Sets up a question for the reader to think 'what is this about'

IT'S remarkable just how bureaucrats and policy-wonks can get it so wrong.

Just this week we published a story about a University of Otago study that shows fewer children are walking to school.

For a variety of reasons more parents are choosing to drop their kids off in the car than let them enjoy some much-needed exercise.

With staggering rises in the number of obese children and adults, which some respected commentators say is a national health crisis, few children walking to their school is enough of a concern.

But the possibility of Taranaki alpine clubs having to ditch their open mountain climbs because of bureaucratic bungling and greed is beyond belief.

Here are clubs whose members go out of their way to introduce many to our wonderful mountain, to our great outdoors, and the Department of Conservation wants to penalise them.

The department wants thousands of dollars from the clubs in permits and safety audits.

The clubs have naturally baulked at the idea and admit having to find the extra money could mean the end of climbs to the summit for hundreds of people every year, people who might otherwise be putting their feet up on the couch and preparing to climb into a mountain of TV watching.

National MP Chester Borrows is bang on the money when he questions the motives of those behind the proposed levy.

"DOC have forgotten who they are working for."

Absolutely. And they have forgotten how much these groups contribute in time, effort and money towards keeping aspiring mountain-goers inspired, informed and safe.

Without the annual open mountain climbs, people would be tempted to make the journey themselves, with all the disastrous consequences that entails.

DOC's bid for money is the wrong move at completely the wrong time and a classic example of too much red tape stopping the flow of oxygen to bureaucrats' brains.

People's lives are becoming increasingly sedentary and they, and the organisations who work to inspire them off their bums and outside, should be encouraged, not actively discouraged.

Rather than having to pay for the privilege of guiding us up our great mountain, the alpine clubs and the tireless members who make up their number should be paid for the contribution they make to the greater good.

Maybe they could take the bureaucrats and bean counters up there.

The fresh air would help clear their heads.

Slang

Colloquial

Emotive exaggeration

Unnamed source

Beginning with a conjunction

Cliche
Slang
Alliteration

Repetition
Personal pronoun

Cliche

Quotation

Minor sentence

Alliteration

Cliche/ metaphor

Slang

Repetition of instruction

Cliche

Metaphor

ISBN 9780170244220

YOU DO:

1 These two texts are quite different in style. Explain the difference in:

- headline

- vocabulary

- use of expert opinion

- use of concrete facts

2 Why is the editorial so different from the article? Think about intended purpose and intended audience.

ISBN 9780170244220

What's next?

By now you will have some idea about how authors use different techniques to create a specific style to achieve their purpose. So, how does all this relate to you and sitting an external assessment on unfamiliar text?

Basically you need to be able to analyse a passage before you begin to answer the questions. It is a matter of being proactive rather than reactive. When you read for pleasure, you read to find out what it is all about. When you read for analysis, you have to do **more** than just read ... **you have to think at the same time**. It is not enough to read a passage for content only. You need to be alert to the techniques being used by the writer.

Here is a passage from a work of fiction, a novel. Read the passage carefully.

Over the next hundred kilometres I watched in dismay as all my determination for a new life drained away as surely as if someone had pulled the plug. I tried kidding myself it was indigestion from one-and-a-half mouthfuls of apple pie, but by the time I spotted the sign for Riverdale School, my gut was churning with fear. In two days all my friends – and now I'd left them behind, they seemed so many and so brilliant – would be back in Year Thirteen at High. And here was I in the middle of nowhere, in the company of assorted farm animals, acres of grass, and a bunch of snooty girls. I longed to be in the city, fighting for a locker, grabbing a battered desk next to Daisy, yelling witty insults down the stair well, sharing my cheese sandwiches and views on Life under the pohutukawa trees. It hadn't occurred to me until this minute that to start a new life you had to ditch the old one. And right now the old one felt like the most precious thing I had. But then, poor Dad, he was going back to the old life – work, garden, Gran on Sunday afternoons – the old life, but without me. And without Mum. I wound down the window, trying to clear my head. I was coming to Riverdale because I'd thought it was what Dad wanted – to be on his own, to get me out of his hair. But what if he was bringing me here because he thought it was what I wanted – to get away from him? I stifled a desperate sob.

Dad nosed the car down a wooded drive and pulled up in front of a three storey brick building smothered in ivy. There was a circular lawn in front with a statue of some pompous old bloke, and a vast spreading tree. At High the statue would have been tagged, the old bloke obscenely defaced. Here, everything was so clean and neat and classy, I already felt like an urchin in my jeans and ratty sweatshirt.

Love and Other Excuses, Jane Westaway

Before you go further ...

1 Complete the following chart.

What is it **about**?	Who is the **audience**?	What is the **style**?	What is the **purpose**?

2 Re-read the passage, and using a highlighter, highlight the different features of language you can see that the author has used. If you need help, refer back to the chart on page 12.

ISBN 9780170244220

At this point, you are half-way there ...

You have read and analysed a passage, which is great. You have thought about it in terms of the big picture. Remember that an external assessment will require you to explain your understanding of the writer's skills and how those skills achieve the writer's purpose.

When you have made some general decisions about the text, you will move into familiar territory. All you have to do is answer the questions, just as you were taught to do in Years 9 and 10.

Having looked at the passage as a whole, you should now find the questions very straightforward to answer.

On the surface

1 What was the narrator's feeling towards the new school? Support your answer with evidence from the text.

2 Give several pieces of information about the narrator of this passage.

3 Give THREE examples from the passage of how Riverdale School is different from High.

Example one:

Example two:

Example three:

ISBN 9780170244220

Technical

4 Write down TWO images used in the passage and, in your own words, explain what each one means.

Image one:

Explanation:

Image two:

Explanation:

Search and think

5 In lines 15–18 the narrator has a dilemma. In your own words, explain what it is.

6 What does the word 'pompous' in line 21 mean?

ISBN 9780170244220

Now let's have a look at the answers and how we got them from the passage.

1 What was the narrator's feeling towards the new school? Support your answer with evidence from the text.

The girl is sad about starting school. She doesn't want to go.

It should have been obvious that the girl is in no way positive about starting the new school. The word 'dismay' in line 1 and 'desperate sob' from line 18 tell you that the narrator is more than 'sad' about the new school. Try and think beyond short, simple words to explain yourself. Also note that this answer does not refer to the second half of the question (support your answer with evidence ...). If you do not answer the question entirely you will not succeed. This student wasted a chance at an Achieve grade.

2 Give **several** pieces of information about the narrator of this passage.

The narrator is starting a new school – Riverdale School. The narrator is female as she is going to a 'snooty' girls school. She is Y13.

The question asks for 'several' pieces of information so you should give more than two. Some of these points could be directly quoted from the text, e.g., 'back in Year Thirteen at High'. Others are inferred, e.g., about her father now being alone 'And without Mum', the country location from 'assorted farm animals' and the private school 'a bunch of snooty girls'. You would have needed to give at least two pieces of information to be awarded the grade.

3 Give **THREE** examples from the passage of how Riverdale School is different from High.

Example one:

There was no 'tagging'.

Example two:

It was 'clean, neat and classy'.

Example three:

It was in the 'country'.

This type of question tests your ability to understand what you read. In this case you needed to skim the passage and look for details that might imply differences rather than state them obviously. You would have needed three clear examples to be awarded a grade.

ISBN 9780170244220

4 Write down **TWO** images used in the passage and, **in your own words**, explain what each one means.

Image one: *'...determination for a new life drained away as surely as if someone had pulled the plug.'*

Explanation: *When a plug is pulled all the water disappears – this is how she sees her commitment to her change of direction in life.*

Image two: *'I already felt like an urchin in my jeans and ratty sweatshirt.'*

Explanation: *An urchin is usually someone who lives in the street or is poor. She feels like this because everything else is so flash and 'rich'.*

An image is any picture created by words used in the passage. Always look for similes and metaphors as they are obvious. 'In your own words' means you must not repeat words already used in the passage. The marker would have expected you to get each part of this answer correct. The 'explanation' requires you to unpack the image and explain what the writer meant literally.

5 In lines 15–18 the narrator has a dilemma. **In your own words**, explain what it is.

She isn't sure if she is attending the new school because her father doesn't want her around any more OR because her father thinks she doesn't want to be living with him.

The question directed you to certain lines from the passage. It is important that you carefully read the appropriate lines several times before you answer the question. The word 'dilemma' implies there is a choice to be made, therefore your answer needs two parts. Sometimes it can be tricky to rephrase the writing in the text.

6 What does the word 'pompous' in line 21 mean?

Pompous means that the person is a snob or thinks they are important.

The question asks for a synonym (a word that has a similar meaning). It is important that you think of the context the word is being used in. See page 44 of this book.

ISBN 9780170244220

An aside on ... answering 'how' questions

We wanted to take some time to stop and look at this little word that seems to trip up a lot of students. Some of the higher level questions will begin with the phrase ... 'How does the author ...?' These are style questions. They don't ask for *what* is said i.e. the content of the text, but how the author gets the content/message across. The 'how' translates to 'what techniques did the author use to make this happen?' In these questions you must talk about techniques ... whether they be parts of speech, figures of speech, punctuation, sentence structures, vocabulary... etc.

An aside on ... answering short-answer questions

- Read the question carefully. Ensure you understand exactly what is being asked of you. If they have not already been highlighted, underline key words.
- Watch for the following phrases:

  In your own words ... this means you cannot copy straight from the text but need to reword your answer.

  Give the word ... if the question asks for a specific number of words make sure that is all you give.

  Quote part of the sentence ... quoting means you need to copy the exact words from the passage. If they ask for part of a sentence, choose only the part that answers the question. Writing the whole sentence may see you lose marks.

  In full sentences ... if you are asked for your answers to be in full sentences, do not use note form.

- If you are unsure of what answer to put down, incorporate all the information you have that relates directly to the question. That way you have covered all bases.
- The number of lines provided for the answer is a clue to how detailed your response needs to be. Try to make more than one point and give more than one example – especially if you are aiming for 'Excellence'.
- Always give a full answer – no credit is given for half an answer.
- If you have been asked to identify a poetic technique or a particular word, you must underline the specific words in the sentence you copy. This shows that you actually know the technique and have not just taken a guess. An entire phrase or sentence that includes but does not highlight the technique will not be rewarded.
- It is important that you know the terminology and can use it to explain yourself clearly.
- Many questions will allow you to score an Achieved, Merit or Excellence from your answer. A clue would be that the first thing that pops into your head is probably **NOT** the Excellence answer! Think ... mull ... expand ... quote ...

An aside on ... answering paragraph questions

When you are asked to write a paragraph answer in close reading, think about what you know from your formal writing. It's essentially the same. Make your point, explain your point and back it up with examples from the text. Then, to get that elusive Excellence, show your response to the text by explaining what you have been made to think by the passage, or what your opinion of the passage's effectiveness is. It will depend on the question, but if you can show that you have been *thinking*, you'll get better results.

ISBN 9780170244220

Written text

Call us old fashioned, but the best way for you to get better at close reading, particularly the analysis part, is to practise.

This section allows you to practise the skills that you have learnt on a variety of unfamiliar texts.

Practice text 1

Read the passage carefully.

Greasies to go ...

The search is on for the hottest fish'n'chips in the country

Next time you lift a chip to your trembling, anticipatory lips, pause and consider what you're about to pop into your mouth. Hold that deep-fried finger of potato up to the light and consider its heft, its colour, its confidence.

Is it a crisp and outstanding chip? Or is it a droopy, greasy, unlovable poor excuse of a thing?

And what of its big friend in the golden overcoat? Is that piece of fish all it should be?

Is it fresh and white, moist and flaky? Or is it a battered soul, a snapper that has long since lost its snap, a lemon fish gone tart? And what about the batter? The batter is a whole other universe.

The judges of this year's Best New Zealand Fish & Chip Shop Competition were taking the batter a bit for granted at their annual rule-setting meeting at a semi-secret meeting in central Auckland a few weeks back. But after long and often intense consideration, batter – or 'coating' as they decided to call it – was given due billing in the taste-judging aspects of the contest, alongside the fish and the chips.

There are 2500 fish and chip shops in New Zealand but only one can be declared New Zealand's best. Apart from the immediate accolades, the winner can expect business to rise by 30 or 40 per cent. Or even more.

But the past three winners of the coveted Best Chippie (if I may abbreviate) Award weren't famous for their big servings, one of the veteran judges revealed. They were famous for the crispy nowness and tastebud-titivating qualities of their ordinary, old-fashioned fish and chips.

Last year's winner, the Westshore Fish Cafe at Bay View, north of Napier, is now coping with a 50 per cent increase in business.

This year's winner is in the process of being decided by a faceless panel of judges who know their oil, their fish, their spuds and their batter, too. And they have high expectations of the things that can happen when those items are brought together with intense heat and wrapped up in paper, all crispy, and taken away for instant consumption.

The competition encourages non-greasiness. In the comprehensive guide sent out to all participating shops, it instructs that thin and crinkly chips are nothing but grease traps (their phrasing is slightly different). Favour 'thick and straight', it says.

The judges will also consider service, variety of menu and décor as they analyse, eliminate and narrow down entrants, secretly sampling 'one scoop chips, one standard fish'.

To avoid suspicion, the judges will look like almost anyone and buy their orders at lunchtime. They'll also be looking at how they're wrapped. Double wrapping is good.

ISBN 9780170244220

Before you go further ...

1 Complete the following chart.

What is it **about**?	Who is the **audience**?	What is the **style**?	What is the **purpose**?

2 Re-read the passage and, using a highlighter, select the different features of language you can see that the author has used. If you need help, refer back to the chart on page 12.

Now answer the following questions in as much detail as possible.

On the surface

1 Quote part of a sentence from lines 26-37 that shows what the judges will be sampling.

2 In your own words explain what the past three winners of the award were famous for.

3 In your own words explain why thin and crinkly chips are out of favour.

Technical

4 Explain the pun in the title sentence.

5 Why have the apostrophes been used in the phrase 'fish'n'chips' (title sentence)?

6 Find an example of a metaphor in lines 1-10.

7 'The batter is a whole other universe' (line 10) is an example of what language feature?

ISBN 9780170244220

8 Comment on the sentence structure of lines 6-10, 'And what of its ... whole other universe.'

9 Why has the word 'coating' (line 14) been placed in inverted commas?

10 Why have brackets been used in the following sentence? 'But the past three winners of the coveted Best Chippie (if I may abbreviate) Award weren't famous for their big servings, one of the veteran judges revealed.'

11 The word 'greasies' (title), 'chippie' (line 20) and 'spuds' (line 27) are examples of what language style?

12 Explain what a compound word is and list TWO examples from the passage.

Search and think

13 Why are the judges considered to be 'faceless'?

COMMENT...

EXPLAIN...

DESCRIBE...

At this level these generally mean the same thing:

write about it.

You might have noticed that there are no grades attached to the questions in this book.

WHY?

Because at this stage you are learning the skills of close reading, rather than worrying about the final grade.

ISBN 9780170244220

Practice text 2

Read the passage carefully.

Routeburn

'This place is turning into a suburban walkway,' lamented the grey-bearded man next to me. 'A few more years, mate, and they won't have to maintain this track – they'll sweep it!'

From our vantage point high above Harris Saddle, the alpine section of the Routeburn Track sprawled before us like a highway, shimmering in December heat. Brightly coloured centipedes of walkers passed each other along the trail and wrapped themselves around the brown steel Harris Saddle shelter shaped like a miniature airport hangar. Someone yodelled, and the tussock meadows rippled with laughter and more or less successful imitations. My companion, an old-fashioned Kiwi tramper dressed in blue-checked Swanndri and green rugby shorts, snorted in disgust. He hadn't walked the track for 20 years, and what he saw now wasn't tramping as he knew it.

The 39-kilometre-long Routeburn straddles the spine of the Humboldt Mountains, which mark the border between Fiordland and Mount Aspiring National Parks. It is the busiest transalpine artery in New Zealand, and yet, some say, still the most beautiful. Whether a result of slick advertising or word of mouth over pizza and cheap wine at backpackers' hostels, its popularity has reached astonishing proportions.

Every year the Routeburn attracts more than 10,000 visitors. They burn seven tonnes of coal and 2000 kg of gas, use nearly 3000 rolls of toilet paper and keep six seasonal staff frantically busy. In summer, the car parks at both ends of the track can resemble parking lots of a good-size supermarket as scores of trampers and day-walkers window-shop for nature's treasures.

Despite their strong outdoors tradition, New Zealanders make up only a quarter of the total number of visitors. Promoted as a major destination by the tourism industry, the Routeburn has become so dominated by foreigners that local trampers are beginning to feel like strangers in their own backyard.

And that backyard is starting to show a few cracks. Local or foreign, thoughtful and nature-loving as they might be, the walkers have brought problems: overcrowded huts, illegal camping, rubbish and the threat of giardia. Most of all, they have endangered the elusive sense of wilderness, the very reason for their visit.

The heart of the problem is that the boom in visitor numbers – in all the national parks, not just Fiordland – has not been matched by government expenditure to maintain and improve facilities. It is only the tolerance of visitors and the ingenuity of track staff which have kept the Routeburn functioning more or less successfully. Now, as demand for the Routeburn and her sister tracks continues to increase, new ways of managing the human torrent are being put in place.

New Zealand Geographic

ISBN 9780170244220

Before you go further ...

1 Complete the following chart.

What is it **about**?	Who is the **audience**?	What is the **style**?	What is the **purpose**?

2 Re-read the passage and, using a highlighter, select the different features of language you can see that the author has used. If you need help, refer back to the chart on page 12.

Answer the following questions in as much detail as possible.

On the surface

1 Why does the Routeburn track resemble 'a surburban walkway' (line 1)?

2 How has the track's popularity grown?

3 Why do local trampers feel like strangers?

4 List FIVE problems caused by the visitors.

ISBN 9780170244220

Technical

5 Explain the metaphor 'centipedes of walkers' (line 6).

6 How is the Routeburn Track compared with the human body? (paragraph 3)

7 The writer uses a metaphor to suggest that numbers of visitors are overwhelming. What is the metaphor?

Search and think

8 Explain what 'that backyard' (line 29) is referring to.

9 In your own words explain how the writer has used both information and emotion in the passage to convey his ideas.

You will notice that from now on, the questions are no longer divided into three sections for you because Year 11 assessment will be a mixture of these question types.

Practice text 3

Read the passage carefully. It is the beginning of a magazine article written about Sam Morgan before he sold Trade Me.

Hello. My name is Mike and I'm a recovering Trade Me addict.

In the last 12 months I've bought a designer coffee pot, two kayaks, a VW Barbie, a pair of ski boots, a Che Guevara box, a spice grinder, a Thunderbirds 2 torch and an orange bikini.

I was doing fine until recently when I bought a Vespa fridge magnet. Okay, two of them.

I now realise I'm not completely safe on my own with a laptop and Trade Me link. But I know there are thousands of others like me out there, battling the same sin.

And I also know the guy who's to blame.

His name's Sam Morgan, he's sharp, smart, probably pretty rich and only 29. What he started in his bedroom is now shared by a million New Zealanders. Trade Me is an internet site where people put things up for sale and others bid for it. It's simple, free and anyone on a computer can get involved. Stuff for sale can be new or used, from a baby's bib to an Auckland apartment, a moped to a Maserati.

It's called an online auction site but this isn't about number babbling and gavel whacking. It's more the 21st century version of the garage sale, a church jumble sale somewhere in cyberspace. It's become New Zealand's busiest website (with 20 million traders predicted this year).

And the country's fastest-growing company, according to the last Deloitte Fast 50 survey – revenue screaming up by 1200 per cent over the last two years, like a Lamborghini with the clutch dropped.

Sam Morgan doesn't flinch at the numbers any more. The exponential upwards sweep of users, sales and revenue has been pure accountancy aerobatics, staggering increase upon staggering increase.

But go to find Morgan and you won't enter a world of chrome and Gucci. The lift to Trade Me central in a Stalinesque Wellington office block lumbers like a Lada, heavy doors heaving open to reveal Trade Me signage and not a lot else. No faux-blonde secretary chirrups 'How may I help you?' because there's no reception desk – just a display of auction paraphernalia, including a Starsky and Hutch cap, a paint-by-numbers version of Van Gogh's Sunflowers, some false eyelashes and a 45 of Mario Lanza rumbling Christmas carols.

There's no nameplate on a smoked glass door saying General Manager because Morgan doesn't have an office. In a sea of corporate youth, he sits in the middle of 40 other workers in scrunched tee shirt and Levis. His number two haircut betrays a ginger tinge, while fading freckles and unconvincing stubble betray his age.

He says 'wicked … cool …. sweet' and it doesn't jar like it would from your average crusty company head.

72 NORTH & SOUTH JUNE 2005

ISBN 9780170244220

Before you go further ...

1 Complete the following chart.

What is it **about**?	Who is the **audience**?	What is the **style**?	What is the **purpose**?

2 Re-read the passage and, using a highlighter, select the different features of language you can see that the author has used. If you need help refer back to the chart on page 12.

Answer the following questions in as much detail as possible.

1 Why does the article begin with the 'handwritten' words? Does the article continue this style?

2 Find TWO examples of similes that use a car image. Explain why they are effective.

3 Using information from paragraphs 4,5 and 6 explain how the writer knows Sam Morgan is not the typical corporate businessman.

4 What is the writer's attitude towards Sam Morgan and his business? Select TWO phrases that show this attitude.

ISBN 9780170244220

Practice text 4

Read the passage carefully.

sunday service

so gay

Steve Braunias explores a strange new slander among our nation's kids

Mr and Mrs Beckham, parents of three: so gay PHOTOGRAPH: AFP

Reading is gay. Maths is gay. The headmaster is totally gay. Morning playtime is gay and so is the food your parents give you for lunch. That dumb shirt – gay. Those awful shoes – gay. Little sisters? Gay. Little brothers? So gay that they may as well be little sisters. Parents do their best, but the plain fact of the matter is that Mum and Dad – inevitable, really, with their nagging and their appalling ignorance of the best things in life – are almost always gay.

Gay is the new insult, the new slander among our nation's kids. How new? Actually, it's kind of old. It seems to have crept into New Zealand about four, five years ago, and has since spread across intermediate schools like moss. It's also in use at primary school and college, but the word peaks with kids aged 11-13. "That's so gay," they announce. "Soooooo gay".

By gay, the mean: lame, stupid, uncool, false, wrong, useless, idiotic, irrelevant, phoney. To be gay is to be rewarded with the highest scorn and contempt. More intelligent users will horse around with the word; for example, "Mr Morris is the ultimate in gay technology." Or: "The gaiety of the speech by Mr Morris was overwhelming." Studies, incidentally, show that most people called Morris are so gay.

What a curious business. Why have they latched onto that particular term? In the lexicon of the 12-year-old New Zealander, gay no longer means gay. They have stripped the word of its sexuality. Really, they have stripped the word of this power.

Gay pride, gay rights, gay lifestyle – that means nothing any more. The gay movement, which worked so hard to find a place in mainstream life, has been stopped in its tracks by brats. They have put a whoopee cushion under it, subverted it, given it another shape.

Why has it taken such particular hold with kids that age? The fact is that no one can identify what's lame, stupid, uncool, false, wrong, useless, idiotic, irrelevant, and phoney with the accuracy and daring of a 12-year-old. Teenagers are too busy posing; adults are past it. At 12, you occupy a state of grace. Childhood, with its giddiness and its toys, is over. The noise of adolesencebangs like a distant drum. At 12, you are in-between – literally, at an intermediate stage.

The body is in revolt, but even more tumultuous change is taking place in the brain, because 12 is the age with the brain makes it debut. A 12-year-old mind is as shiny as a new coin. It flips in the air and makes an instant judgement call – it can tell in a flash what or who is and is not so gay.

Most celebrities are so gay. David Beckham is so gay. Tom Cruise is so gay. Paris Hilton is so gay. In New Zealand, Matthew Ridge, Paul Holmes and Nicky Watson are so gay. The kids know these things. At 12, they are gifted with fabulous insight. Their convictions are strong, their faith is infinite. They have so few distractions. No one takes them seriously. They can't drive, they can't drink. Sex is a private affair. Homework, which is gay, hardly takes up much of their time – they are unburdened by the pressure of crucial exams. Essentially, they are left alone, half-human, half-savage, quite pure.

All well and good, and please excuse the rampant stereotyping of children aged 12. But what to make of the choice of the word gay? It almost certainly arrived on our shores from the US. American online magazine Salon ran a story about it back in 2000. Seven years ago, according to the report, the term was used among adults; Salon argued that it merely "evoked childhood", and was entirely innocent, something to be encouraged.

Really? Last month, the term came before a judge in California. When classmates teased a 13-year-old schoolgirl about her Mormon upbringing ("Do you have 10 moms?"), she responded with the withering put-down: "That's so gay". The principal gave the girl an official warning. Her parents have sued the school. They say the warning has violated her First Amendment rights. They are also – this is so gay – seeking "unspecified damages." The school says the girl was using hate speech. Its lawyers told the court, "We have a duty to protect gay students from harassment ... In furtherance of this goal, prohibition of the phrase 'That's so gay' was a reasonable regulation." The judge will make her ruling next month.

Only in America, probably. But in prim, anxious New Zealand, the use of the term is waiting for trouble. Actually, it has already attracted a complaint to the Broadcasting Standards Authority. Last year, a kid on TV One programme Top of the Class announced that playing the recorder was "extremely gay". Paul Davies complained, saying it would encourage kids to think "gay is bad". The authority ruled that it didn't breach broadcasting standards.

Soon, though, gay will be the old black. Language picks up, discards, moves on. A new expression of scorn and contempt will be needed and seized on without adult supervision or approval. It could well be that anyone lame, stupid, uncool etc will wake up one day in the near future and hear the withering put-down: "You're so het."

Email: stephen.b@star-times.co.nz

ISBN 9780170244220

Before you go further ...

1 Complete the following chart.

What is it **about**?	Who is the **audience**?	What is the **style**?	What is the **purpose**?

2 Re-read the passage and, using a highlighter, select the different features of language you can see that the author has used. If you need help, refer back to the chart on page 12.

Answer the following questions in as much detail as possible. Tackle the three basic questions first, which should expand on what you have written in the grid above.

1 What is the subject of this article?

2 Who is the audience?

3 What is the style of the writing?

Now go on to examine how the writer achieves these outcomes. Answer these next two questions about the passage.

4 Look at the opening paragraph of the article. What techniques have the writer and the magazine used to gain the reader's attention?

ISBN 9780170244220

5 Find one example of a simile, a metaphor, three examples of colloquial language, one example of irony and two examples of hyperbole used in the writing. Explain the effect of each technique.

Simile: ____________________

Effect: ____________________

Metaphor: ____________________

Effect: ____________________

Colloquial language (x3): ____________________

Effect: ____________________

Irony: ____________________

Effect: ____________________

Hyperbole: ____________________

Effect: ____________________

Finally, think about the author's opinion, and your own opinion.

6 Does the writer care about the way the word 'gay' is being used? What does he predict will happen to the word?

7 What do you think about this topic? Have you used the word in this way? Do you still? Should we be worried about the way the meaning of words is changing?

ISBN 9780170244220

Practice text 5

Read the passage carefully. This extract is the opening of a novel. It sets a scene and introduces a character. As this is a more complex text, we are going to help by annotating the passage. These highlights, notes and comments are what your teacher would be discussing with you about the passage.

Setting
Personification
Use of comma makes you pause, go slowly over the o sounds.

Onomatopoeia

Baffled with vacuously: sense of pointless life?

One sentence paragraph. Alliteration. Sense of foreboding.

Alliteration. Quicker pace than opening para. Thrilled = emotive

Short sentences again add detail

Verbs: action
Laterite = reddish clay

Introduces a character. Tense changed. From always to this particular time.

Alliteration, Metaphor, Simile, Physical verb – slammed

In contrast

Minor sentence

Repetition of still. Links to Rahel coming *back*.

From *The God of Small Things,* **by Arundhati Roy**

Paradise Pickles and Preserves

May in Ayemenem is a hot, brooding month. The days are long and humid. The river shrinks and black crows gorge on bright mangoes in still, dustgreen trees. Red bananas ripen. Jackfruit burst. Dissolute bluebottles hum vacuously in the fruity air. Then they stun themselves against clear windowpanes and die, fatly baffled in the sun.

The nights are clear but suffused with sloth and sullen expectation.

But by early June the south-west monsoon breaks and there are three months of wind and water with short spells of sharp glittering sunshine that thrilled children snatch to play with. The countryside turns an immodest green. Boundaries blur as tapioca fences take root and bloom. Brick walls turn mossgreen. Pepper vines snake up electric poles. Wild creepers burst through laterite banks and spill across the flooded roads. Boats ply in the bazaars. And small fish appear in the puddles that fill the PWD potholes on the highways.

It was raining when Rahel came back to Ayemenem. **S**lanting **s**ilver ropes **s**lammed into loose earth, ploughing it up like gunfire. The old house on the hill wore its steep, gabled roof pulled over its ears like a low hat. The walls streaked with moss, had grown soft, and bulged a little with dampness that seeped up from the ground.

The wild, overgrown garden was full of the whisper and scurry of small lives. In the undergrowth a rat snake rubbed itself against a glistening stone. Hopeful bullfrogs cruised the scummy pond for mates. A drenched mongoose flashed across the leaf-strewn driveway.

The house itself looked empty. The doors and windows were locked. The front verandah bare. Unfurnished. But the skyblue Plymouth with chrome tailfins was still parked outside, and inside, Baby Kochamma was still alive.

Metaphor, Contrast, Emotive language: gorge, dustgreen

Short sentences create images.

Words to look up: dissolute (overindulging, harming oneself), vacuously (pointless, unintelligent).

Fruity sums up previous words.

Immodest? (exposing things usually covered). New growth appearing everywhere, not hidden.

Metaphor - visual

Begins with a conjunction – why? Final sentence of description.

Personification

Descriptive detail

Onomatopoeia

Next 3 expand on first sentence.

Explains previous sentence more.

ISBN 9780170244220

Before you go further ...

1 Complete the following chart.

What is it **about**?	Who is the **audience**?	What is the **style**?	What is the **purpose**?

2 Re-read the passage and, using a highlighter, select the different features of language you can see that the author has used. If you need help, refer back to the chart on page 12.

Answer the following questions in as much detail as possible.

1 In your own words, describe the scene set by the opening paragraph. Discuss some of the techniques the writer has used to create this scene. Is it an effective opening?

2 The third paragraph deals with a different month. How does the writer show the differences between May and June?

3 Choose an effective figure of speech that you have not mentioned so far, and explain why it is effective.

4 Choose a part of speech that you have not mentioned so far, and explain why it is effective.

5 In paragraph 4 the tense changes. How? Why?

ISBN 9780170244220

6 Which words in paragraphs 4 and 5 tell you that Rahel has been here before?

7 How does the beginning of paragraph 5 contrast with what has been said in paragraph 4?

An aside on ... emotive language

Emotive language is the deliberate use of words to exaggerate, describing a subject or an event to interest the reader or listener in a way that will excite the emotions.

Emotive words are used extensively in persuasive writing and speaking to convince others of an author's point of view, often on a controversial issue. They express bias, a tendency towards a particular point of view or preference.

There are many examples of emotive language in today's print media and in advertising e.g. controversial headlines in newspapers or suggestive ones in women's magazines, political writing that captures the opinion of the electorate, persuasive letters to the editor, or charity appeals. Talkback radio callers with strong opinions often use highly emotive language, too.

Ordinary word	Emotive word/s
Changed	transformed, mutated, revolutionised
Actor	celebrity, star, ham
Old person	elder, pensioner, kuia, senior citizen
Killed	slaughtered, put to sleep, euthanased
Fire	blaze, inferno, conflagration, bonfire

Try to think of some more emotive ways of saying:

Injured ______
Light ______
Sad ______
Thin ______
Intelligent ______

YOU DO:

John Key, as Leader of the National Party, wrote this emotive item to express one political party's views in the newspaper. We have selected some of his emotive words for you to think about. Look up any you do not know the meaning of, 'draconian' and 'travesty' for example.

National opposes this **self-serving** and **draconian** bill because it is an **assault** on democracy and free speech in election year.

The legislation widens the regulated election period to an **outrageous** one year in three, so when New Zealanders wake up on January 1 they will be regulated by election campaign rules. It **treats New Zealanders as if they are stupid** and seeks to **shut down** opposing opinion in election year.

It imposes a **shambolic** set of rules that nobody, not even Government ministers, the Prime Minister, nor the agency charged with administering it understands. It imposes a **ridiculous and unworkable** third-party regime on anyone who isn't an MP. And it lets Labour spend **tens of millions** of taxpayer dollars through government department advertising in election year to promote Labour policies and **buy** the election.

In summary, it **screws the scrum** in Labour's favour in election year because it is all about shutting down dissent and getting Labour re-elected. Labour **does not care** that our ability to speak freely and engage in political debate is the **casualty**.

The bill is an **anti-democratic travesty** that attacks the rights of ordinary New Zealanders, because their rights no longer count under a government desperate to win another term. National will **axe** this legislation at the first opportunity.

Clearly the writer is not happy. You will get the message even more clearly if you try reading it aloud with emotion!

ISBN 9780170244220

Poetry

We know that some students really love reading and understanding poetry. We also know that others see a poem more as a crossword puzzle to figure out, and a few even think a poem is something the school's English Department invented to make life difficult for teenagers.

Get over it

At least poems are usually quite short and so you can focus easily on one for a brief time to understand and appreciate it.

We hope that you will find the poems we offer here help you to work out effective ways of approaching other poems given to you to study this year. Your teacher is there to help you – as well as those students in your class who enjoy poetry.

In the past you have probably done a fair bit of labelling techniques that a poet has used in a poem. You may have begun to consider why the poet used those techniques. It is now time, in Year 11, to bring it all together and to look at the poem as a whole and to look at its style.

You have been taken through the process of approaching a poem in Year 9 and 10. If you need a refresher course then go back to pages 54-60 in *How to … Achieve in Year 9* or pages 56-59 in *How to … Achieve in Year 10.*

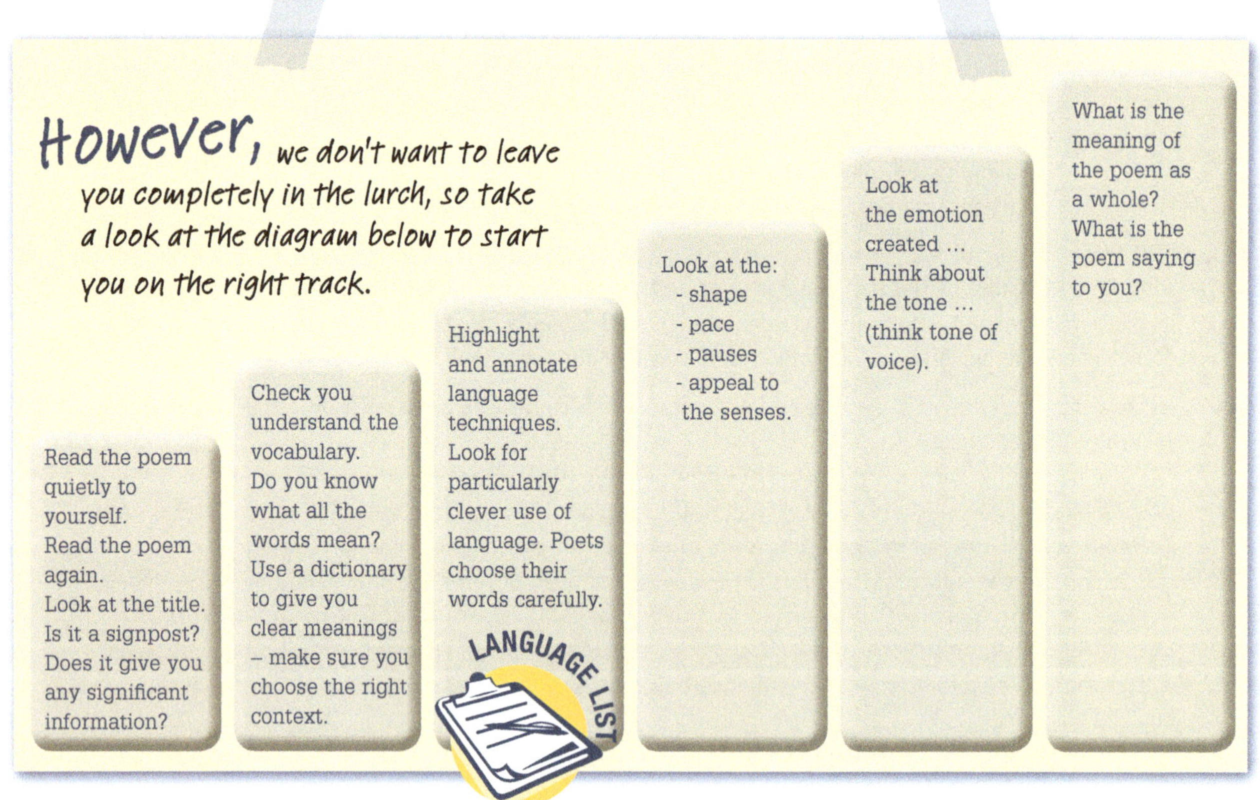

ISBN 9780170244220

Let's work together first …

This poem has been annotated for you to draw your attention to some of its features.

Wintry Gloom

In the cemetery great mossy trees stand naked in the wintry gloom
Their branches **t**wisted and **t**angled like Medusa's hair
They watch the temporary residents pouring out of the city
In angry buses that bully **t**heir way **t**hrough the **t**raffic

Traffic lights shining bright in the half-light create waves of noise
As cars cut the road's wet veneer redistributing the watery film
They race to catch the light cutting deep into the road ahead
Red light reflected onto the wet greasy road struggles to keep up

Wind and rain arrive together turning umbrellas and collars upward
The eyes of those crowded together beneath inadequate shelter do not meet
Uncom**f**ortable with **f**orced intimacy some stand in the rain
Raised hands **f**all in **f**rustration as already **f**ull buses pass (with out) stopping

Later the gloom becomes the dark of night and lamps are haloed by the rain
The noise of people and traffic recedes and the traffic lights signal to nobody
Leaves with membranes like cobwebs have blown into the **g**utter in **g**reat drifts
In the cemetery the city's permanent residents settle in for another night's sleep.

Tommy Gorden

We've helped with the analysis. Now your task is to answer a few questions in as much detail as possible.

1 This New Zealand poem is very descriptive. The poet is asking you to imagine this city scene. Either list the things that you can see, or draw a picture, if you prefer.

ISBN 9780170244220

2 Some punctuation has been left out altogether. Read the poem aloud and put in punctuation marks where you think they are needed.

Now let's look at some of the language chosen by the poet.

3 In the opening line, how does the writer suggest the cemetery is an old place?

4 Why do you think the poet has chosen the simile 'branches twisted and tangled like Medusa's hair'?

5 The poet paints a detailed picture of the wet evening. Choose two examples of personification that add detail to this picture. What do they add to your understanding?

6 Explain who the 'temporary' (line 3) and the 'permanent' (line 16) residents are.

7 What is the central theme of this poem?

ISBN 9780170244220

Let's make a comparison ...

Wintry Gloom is a modern poem describing a winter evening in a city. The next poem was written over a hundred years ago on exactly the same subject. The poet is describing a winter's evening in the early part of the 20th century. You will note that he mentions a cab-horse which tells you the poem is set in the days before buses.

From **Preludes**

The winter evening settles down
With smells of steaks in passageways.
Six o'clock.
The burnt-out ends of smoky days.
And now a gusty shower wraps
The grimy scraps
Of withered leaves about your feet
And newspapers from vacant lots;
The showers beat
On broken blinds and chimney-pots
And at the corner of the street
A lonely cab-horse steams and stamps.
And then the lighting of the lamps.

T.S. Eliot

This poem has a firmly controlled rhythm (count the syllables in the lines to see).

8 Although this poem is set in a car-less era, can you see any similarities in the way T.S. Eliot and Tommy Gorden see a winter evening in the city?

9 What do the following phrases mean to you?

a burnt-out ends

b smoky days

c withered leaves

d broken blinds

e lonely cab-horse ______________________________

____

10 How does T.S. Eliot feel about city life, do you think?

____

____

____

____

____

____

An aside on ... context

It is important to understand that to succeed at this level you will now be expected to answer questions in the context of the whole passage.

Context means the words, phrases and passages that come before and after the words you are being asked about.

For example, it will no longer be enough to just identify a simile and explain that it is comparing two things. You will now need to explain the nature of the simile's point of comparison and relate that comparison to the whole piece.

Let's look at an example. The poet is describing his vessel:

'As idle as a painted ship
Upon a painted ocean'

- We could say the poet is using a simile, comparing his ship to a picture of a ship.
- We could go further and say that the poet is suggesting that the ship is not moving at all.
- Or we could link the idea to the poem (*The Rime of the Ancient Mariner,* by Samuel Taylor Coleridge) as a whole and say that the poet is showing the reader how the mariner feels trapped and powerless on this ship that is supposed to carry him along but is not moving at all, as trapped as if he were on a ship in a painting.

You should be ready to have a go on your own now. Complete the following four practice tasks. You will notice that each poem has been placed on the page so that there is space for you to write your own observations around the poem. Use the boxes to help you. In other words, annotate the poem before you attempt to answer the questions.

ISBN 9780170244220

Practice poem 1

Use a dictionary to look up the following words:

Bric-a-brac *terrapin* *potto*
myna *bicker* *neutered*
dowagers *macaw* *succubus*
whim

Underline any phrases you think are significant. Underline any language techniques you come across. Think about why the poet used them ... what do they add to the image, poem, your understanding?

Pet Shop

Cold blood or warm, crawling or fluttering
Bric-a-brac, all are here to be bought,
Noisy or silent, python or myna,
Fish with long silk trains like dowagers,
Monkeys lost to thought.

In a small tank tiny enameled
Green terrapin jostle, in a cage a crowd
Of small birds elbow each other and bicker
While beyond the ferrets, eardrum, eyeball
Find that macaw too loud.

Here behind glass lies a miniature desert,
The sand littered with rumpled gauze
Discarded by snakes like used bandages;
In the next door desert fossilized lizards
Stand in a pose, a pause.

But most of the customers want something comfy –
Rabbit, hamster, potto, puss –
Something to hold on the lap and cuddle
Making believe it will return affection
Like some neutered succubus.

Purr then or chirp, you are here for our pleasure,
Here at the mercy of our whim and purse;
Once there was the wild, now tanks and cages,
But we can offer you a home, a haven,
That might prove even worse.

Louis MacNeice

ISBN 9780170244220

Answer the following questions in as much detail as possible.

1 What is the poet describing in the first 8 lines of the poem?

2 What image is created in lines 10-11?

3 Comment on the use of alliteration in line 15.

4 Contrast the beginning and end of the poem. Why has the poet chosen to show this difference?

5 Comment on the title of the poem. In your opinion, is it an effective title?

ISBN 9780170244220

Practice poem 3

Underline any phrases you think are significant. Underline any language techniques you come across. Think about why the poet used them ... what do they add to the image, poem, your understanding?

Being Sixteen

It's
Never been easy
Sixteening:
Reading Shakespeare,
Searching for meaning;
Playing different roles
For everyone you've met
Wanting all the applause
You can get.

Feeling guilty
For deeds not done:
Trying to connect with anyone:
Searching for words
With crystal-clear meaning:
Never been easy
Sixteening.

A head that's full
Of new dreams every week,
Like treetops that trap
Morning mist off a creek:
Pushing out feelers
And pulling them in:
Trying to be yourself
While still fitting in:
Standing tall
When your heart's bleeding:
Never been easy
Sixteening.

Michael Khan

ISBN 9780170244220

Answer the following questions in as much detail as possible.

1 The poet chooses to turn 'Being Sixteen' into a verb 'Sixteening'. Can you think why he has done so?

2 Explain these two metaphors in as much detail as possible:

a 'Pushing out feelers/And pulling them in' (lines 21/22)

b 'Standing tall/When your heart's bleeding' (lines 25/26)

3 The poet selects several other things that make life complicated for sixteen-year-olds. What are they? Try to use your own words.

4 Do you agree with the poet? Do you disagree? Why? Explain in detail.

ISBN 9780170244220

Practice poem 4

Use a dictionary to look up the following words:

docile	*animate*
tethered	*terrestrial*

Underline any phrases you think are significant. Underline any language techniques you come across. Think about why the poet used them ... what do they add to the image, poem, your understanding?

Kite

On the beach the waves pour in furiously
The wind lashes the dunes
The bay fills with rain, smoky, and clears
And from the hill's bulk the flax bushes
Shine out suddenly, like many waterfalls.

So fly the yellow kite, a brave flutter
Against the grey and brown. It bucks and
Dives, pulling down hope from the sky.
Behind, the thirty-foot scarlet tail snaps
In the wind, a red scissor of light.

It is a live thing, tugging
At the end of its lines. It is not docile
Like the purple and green dragon kite
Content to sit all day, bobbing as the breeze
Drops and lifts, tethered to the fence.

It cruises, hungry
Very small and spare, animate, fierce
Its one black eye regarding us curiously
Two grayish brown figures, heavy
Terrestrial, shoes full of sand.

Anne French

ISBN 9780170244220

Answer the following questions in as much detail as possible.

1 Emotive words are used in verse 1 to describe the weather. Identify effective words and comment on their use.

2 What does the poet want the reader to notice about the kite in verse 2?

3 Verse 3 compares the yellow kite with another kite. Explain how the poet sees this other kite.

4 In verse 4 the poet describes the yellow kite as if it is alive, with an eye to watch the people on the beach. What is the meaning of this verse?

ISBN 9780170244220

Playing with poetry

Read this famous poem through carefully several times. It's a very good one to read aloud or have read to you. Notice the rhyme and the rhythm. It is called a ***narrative poem*** because it tells a story.

The Lady of Shalott

Part I

On either side the river lie
Long fields of barley and of rye,
That clothe the wold and meet the sky;
And through the field the road runs by
    To many-towered Camelot;
And up and down the people go,
Gazing where the lilies blow
Round an island there below,
    The island of Shalott.

repetition
the prison
colour,
captive
apart from
the world

Willows whiten, aspens quiver,
Little breezes dusk and shiver
Through the wave that runs for ever
By the island in the river
    Flowing down to Camelot.
Four grey walls, and four grey towers
Overlook a space of flowers,
And the silent isle imbowers
    The Lady of Shalott.

she is a
mystery,
makes no
contact with
world
rhetorical
question

By the margin, willow veiled
Slide the heavy barges trailed
By slow horses; and unhailed
The shallop flitteth silken-sailed
    Skimming down to Camelot;
But who hath seen her wave her hand?
Or at the casement seen her stand?
Or is she known in all the land,
    The Lady of Shalott?

Only reapers, reaping early
In among the bearded barley,
Hear a song that echoes cheerly
From the river winding clearly,
    Down to towered Camelot;
And by the moon the reaper weary,
Piling sheaves in uplands airy,
Listening, whispers 'Tis the fairy
    Lady of Shalott.'

Part II

There she weaves by night and day
A magic web with colours gay.
She has heard a whisper say,
A curse is on her if she stay
    To look down to Camelot.
She knows not what the curse may be,
And so she weaveth steadily,
And little other care hath she,
    The Lady of Shalott.

And moving through a mirror clear
That hangs before her all the year,
Shadows of the world appear.
There she sees the highway near
    Winding down to Camelot;
There the river eddy whirls,
And there the surly village-churls,
And the red cloaks of market girls,
    Pass onward from Shalott.

Sometimes a troop of damsels glad,
An abbot on an ambling pad,
Sometimes a curly shepherd-lad,
Or long-haired page in crimson clad,
    Goes by to towered Camelot;
And sometimes through the mirror blue
The knights come riding two and two:
She hath no loyal knight and true,
    The Lady of Shalott.

But in her web she still delights
To weave the mirror's magic sights,
For often through the silent nights
A funeral, with plumes and lights
    And music, went to Camelot;
Or when the moon was overhead,
Came two young lovers lately wed;
'I am half sick of shadows,' said
    The Lady of Shalott.

Part III

A bow-shot from her bower-eaves,
He rode between the barley-sheaves,
The sun came dazzling through the leaves,
And flamed upon the brazen greaves
    Of bold Sir Lancelot.
A red-cross knight for ever kneeled
To a lady in his shield,

ISBN 9780170244220

That sparkled in the yellow field,
    Beside remote Shalott.

The gemmy bridle glittered free,
Like to some branch of stars we see
Hung in the golden Galaxy.
The bridle bells rang merrily
    As he rode down to Camelot;
And from his blazoned baldric slung
A mighty silver bugle hung,
And as he rode his armour rung,
    Beside remote Shalott.

All in the blue unclouded weather
Thick-jewelled shone the saddle-leather,
The helmet and the helmet-feather
Burned like one burning flame together,
    As he rode down to Camelot;
As often through the purple night,
Below the starry clusters bright,
Some bearded meteor, trailing light,
    Moves over still Shalott.

His broad clear brow in sunlight glowed;
On burnished hooves his war-horse trode;
From underneath his helmet flowed
His coal-black curls as on he rode,
    As he rode down to Camelot.
From the bank and from the river
He flashed into the crystal mirror,
'Tirra lirra,' by the river
    Sang Sir Lancelot.

She left the web, she left the loom,
She made three paces through the room,
She saw the water-lily bloom,
She saw the helmet and the plume,
    She looked down to Camelot.
Out flew the web and floated wide;
The mirror cracked from side to side;
'The curse is come upon me,' cried
    The Lady of Shalott.

Part IV

In the stormy east-wind straining,
The pale yellow woods were waning,
The broad stream in his banks complaining,
Heavily the low sky raining
    Over towered Camelot;
Down she came and found a boat
Beneath a willow left afloat,
And round about the prow she wrote
    The Lady of Shalott.

And down the river's dim expanse
Like some bold seer in a trance,
Seeing all his own mischance —
With a glassy countenance
    Did she look to Camelot.
And at the closing of the day
She loosed the chain, and down she lay;
The broad stream bore her far away,
    The Lady of Shalott.

Lying, robed in snowy white
That loosely flew to left and right —
The leaves upon her falling light —
Through the noises of the night
    She floated down to Camelot;
And as the boat-head wound along
The willowy hills and fields among,
They heard her singing her last song,
    The Lady of Shalott.

Heard a carol, mournful, holy,
Chanted loudly, chanted lowly,
Till her blood was frozen slowly,
And her eyes were darkened wholly,
    Turned to towered Camelot.
For ere she reached upon the tide
The first house by the water-side,
Singing in her song she died,
    The Lady of Shalott.

Under tower and balcony,
By garden-wall and gallery,
A gleaming shape she floated by,
Dead-pale between the houses high,
    Silent into Camelot.
Out upon the wharfs they came,
Knight and burgher, lord and dame,
And round the prow they read her name,
    The Lady of Shalott.

Who is this? and what is here?
And in the lighted palace near
Died the sound of royal cheer;
And they crossed themselves for fear,
    All the knights at Camelot;
But Lancelot mused a little space;
He said, 'She has a lovely face;
God in his mercy lend her grace,
    The Lady of Shalott.'

Alfred Lord Tennyson

ISBN 9780170244220

Reading for meaning

1 You should be able to picture what is happening without knowing the meaning of every word, but it is still a good idea to look up any words you do not understand. This may include: *wold, shallop, casement, churls, page, ambling pad, bower-eaves, red-cross knight, gemmy, blazoned baldric, prow, countenance, burgher, grace.*

Annotate the meanings around the poem.

2 Now look at the parts of the poem we have highlighted for you. Each is a technique and/or important detail. Can you identify the techniques and explain the effect or importance of the words? We have completed two for you as a guide to what is expected. You will be able to use these notes as you answer the questions that follow.

SETTING (Time, place and social background all have a bearing on this poem).

3 To show that you can see where the events are taking place and what is happening use this storyboard to draw a picture showing the scene in Parts I, II, III, IV.

Part I	Part II
Part III	Part IV

ISBN 9780170244220

PLOT

A narrative poem tells a story. In your own words briefly explain the plot-line of this poem. Write it in the four parts that the poem is divided into.

Part I ______________________________

Part II ______________________________

Part III ______________________________

Part IV ______________________________

CHARACTER

The Lady is the main character. How does the poet reveal her character? (Ask yourself: does he show what she looks like? What she does? What she says? What she feels? Why she makes her decisions?)

Sir Lancelot is the other named character. How is he described? What is his impact on the Lady? Why does he have this impact? What is his role at the end of the poem?

ISBN 9780170244220

ATMOSPHERE

Think about how the atmosphere changes as the story progresses and how the poet shows these changes. Look particularly at verses 2, 5, 8, 12, 13, 17. Consider colours, rhythm (including length of words), rhyme, sounds, symbols etc.

THEME

What, in your opinion, is the theme of the poem? (You might consider the role of women in Victorian society, the idea of unrequited love, the way an artist or writer can be isolated from the world while painting or writing about life, art vs real experience, romantic tragedy etc.)

Look at this painting which illustrates the poem. Explain what you can see that shows the painter's understanding of the story. In other words, what are the visual-verbal links?

ISBN 9780170244220

Visual text

Some students enjoy studying visual text more than written text. A visual text may seem more straightforward and simple to understand, but don't be fooled into thinking it is easy!

The word Visual might suggest that a visual text is something that is merely seen, but in actual fact it is something that you *read* in the same way as you read a piece of writing.

Visual text are often complex in both their design and their use of language.

HERE IS A Visual

What have you 'read'? List what you can tell about this person from this photograph.

____

____

____

____

ISBN 9780170244220

So how much do you remember?

Seeing as this section is about visual text, we decided to remind you visually of the knowledge and skills you should be bringing to this text type.

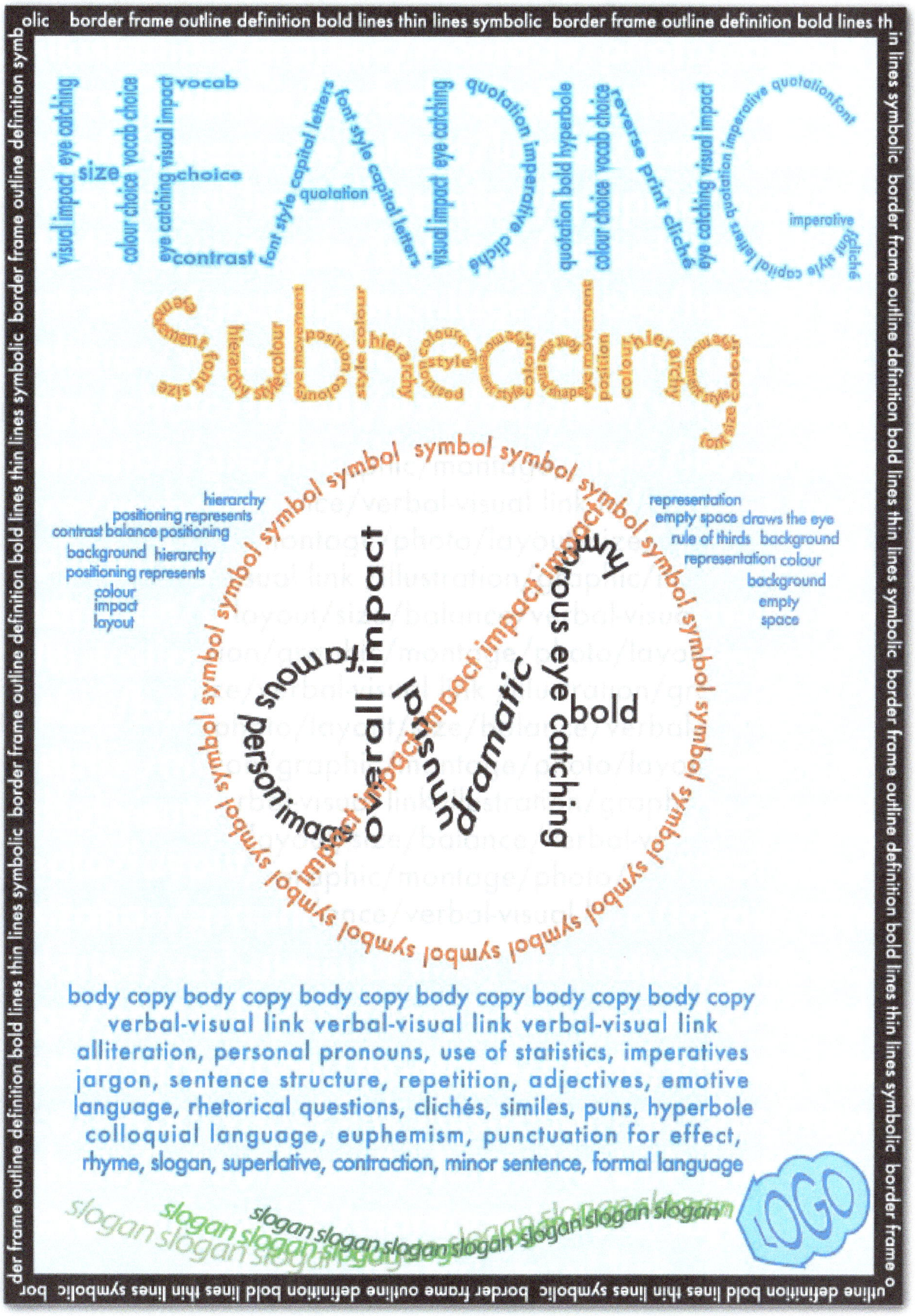

border frame outline definition bold lines thin lines symbolic border frame outline definition bold lines thin lines symbolic

HEADING

visual impact eye catching size colour choice vocab choice eye catching visual impact vocab choice contrast font style capital letters quotation font style capital letters visual impact eye catching quotation imperative cliché quotation bold hyperbole colour choice vocab choice reverse print cliché eye catching visual impact quotation imperative capital letters font style quotation font imperative font style capital letters cliché

Subheading

font size element hierarchy style colour eye movement position colour colour style hierarchy colour style paused hierarchy style colour shape eye movement position colour hierarchy style colour font size

symbol symbol symbol symbol symbol symbol symbol symbol symbol symbol symbol symbol symbol symbol symbol symbol symbol

impact impact impact impact impact impact

famous personimage overall impact unusual dramatic famous eye catching bold

hierarchy
positioning represents
contrast balance positioning
background hierarchy
positioning represents
colour
impact
layout

representation
empty space draws the eye
rule of thirds background
representation colour
background
empty
space

graphic/montage/photo/layout/size/balance/verbal-visual link/illustration/graphic

body copy body copy body copy body copy body copy body copy
verbal-visual link verbal-visual link verbal-visual link
alliteration, personal pronouns, use of statistics, imperatives
jargon, sentence structure, repetition, adjectives, emotive language, rhetorical questions, clichés, similes, puns, hyperbole
colloquial language, euphemism, punctuation for effect,
rhyme, slogan, superlative, contraction, minor sentence, formal language

slogan slogan slogan slogan slogan slogan slogan slogan slogan slogan slogan

LOGO

Let's work together first …

This visual has been annotated for you to draw your attention to some of its features.

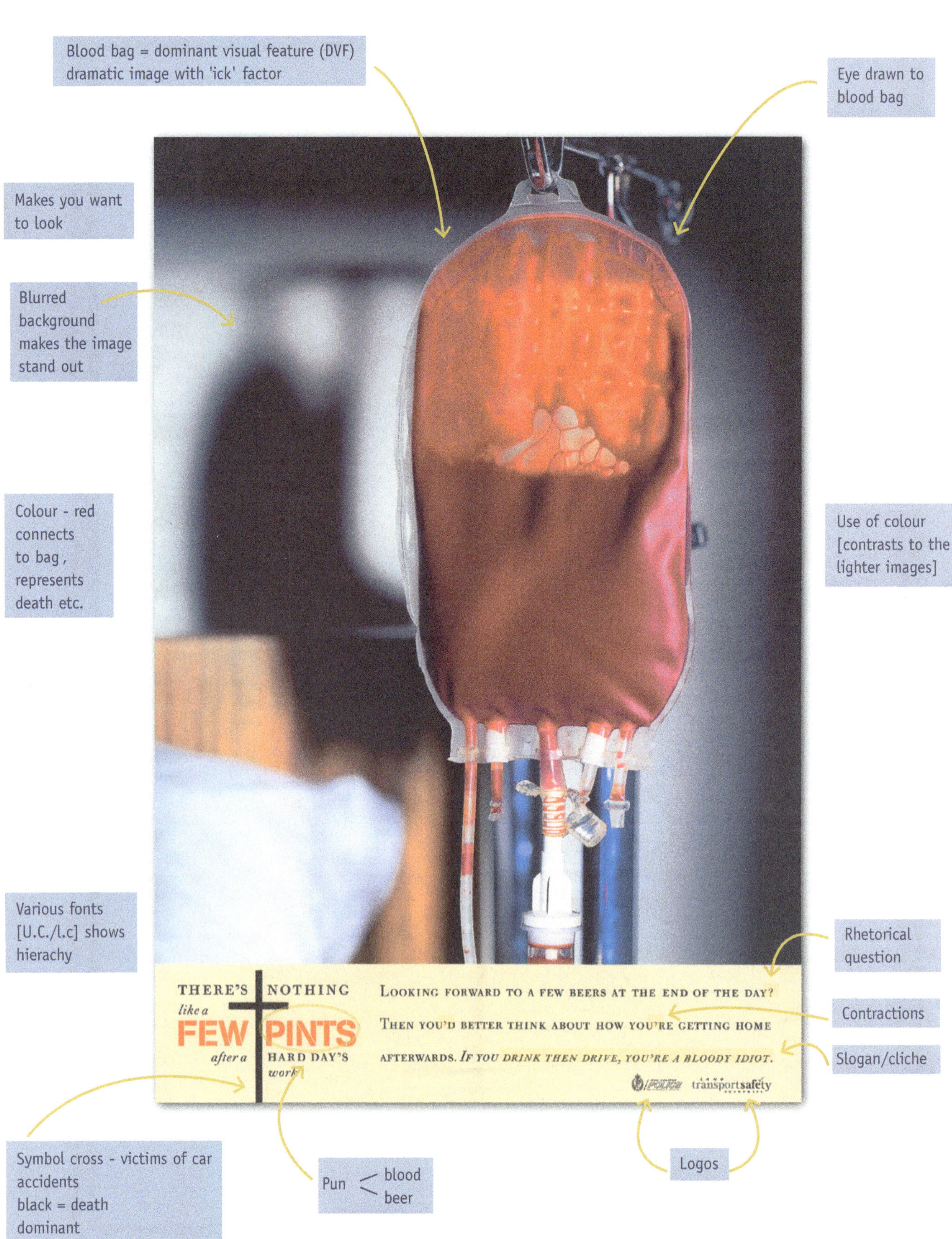

ISBN 9780170244220

Before you go further ...

1 Complete the following chart.

What is it **about**?	Who is the **audience**?	What is the **style**?	What is the **purpose**?

Answer the following questions in as much detail as possible.

1 Why does this advertisement attract attention?

2 What is the intended message of the advertisement?

3 Explain the pun used in this advertisement.

4 The designer of this advertisement has used a symbol. Identify the symbol and explain its purpose.

5 Why has the last sentence in the body copy been written in italics?

ISBN 9780170244220

6 This advertisement has been designed for the viewer's eye to move through the poster starting at the dominant visual feature and ending at the logos. Clearly describe how this movement takes place.

New to you might be ... imperative

When something is 'imperative' it must be done. Therefore, in grammar the word means 'command'. Imperatives are used to give orders, commands and instructions. They are very common in advertising, trying to provoke the consumer into action, for example:

- Buy now!
- Eat at Joe's.
- Shop at Sam's Supermarket.
- Make the right choice – choose Charlie's.

Listen to the TV advertising and you will hear many imperatives. Listen to your parents and you will hear plenty, too.

- Get up now.
- Tidy your room.
- Turn off the TV.
- Finish your homework.
- Go to bed.

An aside on ... the verbal-visual link

Let's take a minute to remind ourselves about the importance of the verbal-visual link.
Whenever a visual text is put together there is always a strong focus on the links that exist between the verbal and the visual elements. Sometimes the link will be obvious at a glance but in other cases the body copy will extend the link further.

Spend a few minutes looking carefully at a visual text. Notice the details in the drawing or the photographs. Read the words. Look around the edges at any logos or borders.

You need to LOOK with your brain as well as your eyes!

ISBN 9780170244220

Practice visual 1

Before you go further …

1 Complete the following chart.

What is it **about**?	Who is the **audience**?	What is the **style**?	What is the **purpose**?

2 Re-read the visual text and, using a highlighter, select and annotate the different features (verbal, visual, layout) you can see.

Answer the following questions in as much detail as possible.

1 Give TWO examples of how balance is created in this static image.

i ______________________________

____

ii ______________________________

____

2 Identify THREE verbal-visual links in this static image.

i ______________________________

____

ii ______________________________

____

iii ______________________________

____

3 Identify ONE visual and ONE verbal feature that link to Maori in this static image.

Visual ______________________________

____

Verbal ______________________________

____

4 Explain why the chosen colours are used in this static image.

____

____

____

5 The body copy ends with an imperative (command). What is it telling us to do?

____

____

____

ISBN 9780170244220

6 What do the two minor sentences – 'Real Treasures. Real Tales.' – suggest about the museum?

____

____

____

Practice visual 2

ISBN 9780170244220

Before you go further ...

1 Complete the following chart.

What is it **about**?	Who is the **audience**?	What is the **style**?	What is the **purpose**?

2 Re-read the visual text and, using a highlighter, select and annotate the different features (verbal, visual, layout) you can see.

Answer the following questions in as much detail as possible.

1 'Completely', 'utterly' and 'indisputably' are all examples of?

2 Why have they chosen to compare the amount of blackcurrants grown to rugby fields?

3 How has balance been used in this image?

4 Explain the pun 'put the Kiwi in New Zealand Ribena'.

5 Why does the company want to sell the fact that the blackcurrants are grown in New Zealand, despite Ribena being made elsewhere?

ISBN 9780170244220

6 Describe the tone of this advertisement.

7 Comment on the choice of colours in this advertisement.

8 How has the designer made this advertisement appealing to the reader? Use evidence to support your answer.

9 List all the connections you can find between the verbal and the visual elements of the advertisement.

Practice visual 3

ISBN 9780170244220

Before you go further …

1 Complete the following chart.

What is it **about**?	Who is the **audience**?	What is the **style**?	What is the **purpose**?

2 Re-read the visual text and, using a highlighter, select and annotate the different features (verbal, visual, layout) you can see.

Answer the following questions in as much detail as possible.

1 Identify the verbal and visual techniques used in the headline (below) of the text.

Don't get stuck inside for the next 40 years!

get fresh

get a future in the dairy industry

Verbal	Visual

2 The reader is encouraged to read through all of this visual text by the careful positioning of words and pictures. Explain the route that the reader's eye takes through this image, e.g. where you should start, where you move to, and why.

a Start with … __________

b … and move to … __________

c … and move to … __________

d … then … __________

e … finally … __________

ISBN 9780170244220

3 This visual text has been designed so that its style will appeal to a youthful market. How does it achieve this?

4 Explain the link between the black and white drawings that form part of background of the image and the words used the image. What is the purpose of these verbal-visual links?

New to you might be ... hyperbole

We wanted to take the time to introduce what may be a new term to many of you. Hyperbole is figurative language where an exaggeration is created to aid imagery. It may be used to show emphasis or make a point in an entertaining way, or it can be used to make fun of someone or something.

Hyperbole is used a lot in humorous poems or light-hearted prose. Comedians also use it to make jokes.

For example:

My sister uses so much makeup that she broke the chisel trying to get it off last night.
My teacher is so old, they have already nailed the coffin shut.
I think of you a million times a day.

YOU DO:

Underline the exaggerated statement in the following sentences:

1 My car is so old, it is pulled by a horse.
2 My grandfather is so slow, I miss two shows when he walks in front of the television.
3 My brother is so tall, he has to duck to walk under the telephone lines.
4 My sister has such long legs, she needs to sit in the backseat to drive.
5 His long legs turned to jelly.

ISBN 9780170244220

On your Own

4

Practice makes perfect

By now you will have spent a fair bit of time honing your Close Reading skills. You will need these skills at the end of the year as your ability to close read will be assessed in the external examinations.

The achievement standard requires reading a range of short texts, or extracts, that you have not previously studied, and writing a response to questions that test your understanding of ideas, style and language features.

In our study of English you close read text often. The difference here is that in an external assessment you will not have the luxury of hearing the piece read by your teacher, discussing the text with your teacher and your classmates or writing your responses in consultation with others. In an external assessment you are on your own.

Of course you cannot consult a dictionary in an assessment, now can you read something aloud, but as you *prepare for* this kind of test use all the tools at your disposal. You might try to understand a text without a dictionary but then use one to explain some vocabulary. This will illustrate to you how important it is to extend you own vocabulary.

1. Make sure that you understand the text.
2. Read the text several times.
3. Check meanings of words that you don't fully understand. Annotate (write on the edge of) the text with your meanings.
4. Annotate the text with notes about what you think the text is saying.
5. Highlight effective use of figurative language.
6. Note down what you think the message/theme of the text is.
7. Add any personal opinions you think about as you read the text. Your personal response is always important.
8. Read each question carefully, highlighting the key words to be sure you answer all parts of the question.
9. Think about and make brief notes about your answer before you begin writing.
10. Essentially you are holding you own private discussion about the text before you begin. Time spent thinking and planning an answer is never a waste of time.

BUT TIME IS IMPORTANT:

External assessments will have time constraints. It is likely you will have an hour to look at a minimum of 3 passages. This give you roughly 20 minutes per passage. Hence why we make you practice so much! The work you put into 'learning' to close read now will help you deal with the pressure of doing the same thing in an assessment environment.

ISBN 9780170244220

Practice 1

Read the poem carefully and answer the questions that follow.

Why Don't You Talk To Me?

Why do I post my love letters in a hollow log?
Why put my lips to a knothole in a tree
And whisper your name?

The spiders spread their nets
And catch the sun,
And by my foot in the dry grass
Ants rebuild a broken city.
Butterflies pair in the wind,
And the yellow bee,
His holsters packed with bread,
Rides the blue air like a drunken cowboy.

More and more I find myself
Talking to the sea.
I am alone with my footsteps.
I watch the tide recede,
And I am left with miles of shining sand.

Why don't you talk to me?

Alistair Campbell

1 Describe the structure of verse 1.

2 Name the creatures that the poet brings to our notice in verse 2. What qualities do the creatures share?

3 Why does the bee remind the poet of a 'drunken cowboy'?

4 Comment on the placement of the last line of the poem and its relevance to the whole poem's meaning.

5 What do you think has happened to make the person in the poem feel this way?

ISBN 9780170244220

Practice 2

Read the passage carefully and answer the questions that follow.

The sea smelt rotten: the waves churning up the sea floor and spitting its contents onto the grey sand. The clouds hung thick and heavy with bits of light lingering in the west. No one was at the beach, thank goodness.

Simon sat for a while seeing nothing, feeling the weight of sadness clinging to him. If he was a girl he would probably cry now but fear had crept inside and sat waiting, though he had no idea what he was afraid of.

Without his beloved drink, Simon was unable to ignore the pain that pressed firmly into his heart. He knew he was hurting others but didn't have the strength to stop himself. He was a coward.

Just like Proctor, who though he might say the thing with Abigail was over, still burned with lust for her. Simon felt just the same way about alcohol. His blessed fog. The grey mist that embraced him, comforted him. All he had to do was walk down to the tavern and pick up a bottle right now and he'd be back in the familiar place.

Simon pulled out his wallet. It was empty. He sighed. Just as well.

He watched someone swimming strongly toward a boat which rocked out in the bay. The strokes were constant, rhythmic and Simon was full of envy. Right now if he tried to do that he would probably drown. He was more at home in an ocean of alcohol.

He turned away. Is that how it was to be? Was that how it was for him? Was the Simon Hassell that used to be, gone, drowned in a hundred bottles of vodka? The pounding waves drummed the questions as he walked along the sand.

Like hell.

He was not going to let his life eke out of him, like Jesse's blood on the road. Sooner or later he would have to face the demons.

Compulsion, Tania Kelly Roxborogh

1 Why was the phrase 'thank goodness' used to end the third sentence?

2 Identify an example of personification and explain what it suggests.

3 In your own words explain why Simon thought he was a coward.

ISBN 9780170244220

4 Why is Simon pleased he has no money?

5 Comment on the connection between the first four lines and the rest of the passage.

An aside on ... tone

If you look up the word 'tone' in a dictionary - and this would be a good idea - you will see that it has many meanings. Some meanings are to do with music, some are to do with sounds, some are to do with colour. In close reading you are using this meaning:

> 'A particular style in discourse or writing, which expresses the person's sentiment or reveals his character; also *spec.* in literary criticism, an author's attitude to his subject matter or audience; the distinctive mood created by this.' (OED)

When you are looking into the tone of a passage or text:

- Consider the vocabulary the writer chooses. Words can have a literal and figurative meanings. All the ones chosen will have been chosen for a purpose.
- Think about the way words and syllables have distinct sounds: hard, soft etc. You will be aware of this when you read poetry. It applies to prose, too.
- Look at the way the words are put together. Long sentences? Short sentences? Does this create any special effects? Is anything missing in the description?
- Are you affected by the words? Do you feel sad? Or happy? Or alarmed? Or surprised? Or persuaded? Or amused? Or...?

These questions should help you to identify the tone of the passage more easily.

ISBN 9780170244220

Practice 3

Read the passage carefully and answer the questions that follow.

Mana Wahine

Now that the Manu Ariki competition is over, the girls have calmed down. But it was an experience never to be forgotten. As soon as I walked through the gates to the powhiri, it was like something entered me, but I didn't know what it was. I was still myself, though. Seeing the groups doing their first waiata, showing off their talents to everyone ... but that was just the powhiri. We still had the whole two days to go yet.

Finally it was time to get the competition on the way. It was ace seeing the groups battling it out on stage, pushing themselves to a higher and higher standard. But the best part for me was when the other groups would stand and tautoko the performing groups. It was like warriors challenging. Dust rising from the ground from the stamping of the takahia, voices carried above and past the hills, eyes lighting up like light bulbs in the dark, and the actions, each with its own meaning.

It was really something. You could see the tears filling the eyes of the crowd. When Turakina stood to perform, we were the centre of attention. Even though I was the guitarist, the crowd could still see every movement I made, so I was very careful.

The waiata we did, especially the haka and our entry, filled the crowd with excitement – and the groups we were competing against with envy. Even on stage as a performer I could see the crowd's eyes light up when they saw Te Kotiro Tuturu in their red, black and white.

We performed like the sea: one moment beautiful and flowing, the next, stamping our feet, working the patu, pulling our lips down, and showing the whites of our eyes. And being inside the shell with our waha nui, the sound effects were like a bomb!

After our performance we were commented on like we were superstars or something. It was massive. Prize-giving came. Groups were in bunches in front of the stage, anxiously waiting for their names to be called out as first prize winners. We didn't win, but came second, and that was massive. It was awesome, too, everyone cheering and clapping, the drumbeats of the Pacific Islanders, and once again the waiata of the groups.

It was finally over: people saying their congratulations, their final goodbyes, hugs and kisses, and I can't forget the tears of the girls. They spread around the two winning roopu, Tuhoe Potiki and Turakina. When we finally got to our bus, girls were still clinging on to their cuzzies and bros making it harder to say goodbye, but finally we unclenched them and headed back to school. On the way back, the girls were singing and doing the haka, never to forget the experience of Manu Ariki.

Terri Hudson, Turakina Maori Girls' College

1 In your own words explain what you understand about the competition.

2 What is the role of the narrator in her group's performance and what is her attitude to her role?

3 In your own words, explain what narrator means when she says 'We performed like the sea' (paragraph 5).

4 The writer uses several other similes in the passage. Choose TWO and explain the effect of each one.

Simile one:

Explanation:

Simile two:

Explanation:

5 How does the language used show the age of the narrator? Give at least THREE examples.

ISBN 9780170244220

Practice 4

Read the poem carefully and answer the questions that follow.

Thistles

Against the rubber tongues of cows and the hoeing
Hands of men
Thistles spike the summer air
Or crackle open under a blue-black pressure.

Every one a revengeful burst
Of resurrection, a grasped fistful
Of splintered weapons and Icelandic frost thrust up

From the underground stain of a decayed Viking.*
They are like pale hair and the gutturals of dialects.
Every one manages a plume of blood

Then they grow grey, like men.
Mown down, it is a feud. Their sons appear,
Stiff with weapons, fighting back over the same ground.

Ted Hughes

*Viking: a member of the Scandinavian people who raided and invaded various parts of northwest Europe from the 8th to the 11th century AD.

Anyone who has fought a battle with thistles in a paddock or garden will understand this poem's meaning.

1 This poem reveals the thistle as a violent presence. How does the poet link the plant to violence? Focus on lines 4-7 and 11-12.

2 The poem creates several images. Explain each one listed here and say how effective it is.

a the rubber tongues of cows

b spike the summer air

ISBN 9780170244220

c crackle open

d a plume of blood

e grow grey, like men

3 Relate this poem to New Zealand.

An aside on … succeeding at Unfamiliar Text

Just to recap, if you wish to achieve this Achievement Standard then you must:

ANSWER THE QUESTION. Read the whole question. Note the key words in the question. Note that 'Identify' and 'Explain' are different instructions: one generally follows the other.

ANSWER ALL THE QUESTIONS. The questions build up a whole picture of your understanding. Don't pick and choose.

WRITE YOUR ANSWER CLEARLY. Take a moment to think it out, even jot down notes, before you write any words at all.

SUPPORT YOUR ANSWER. Quote examples from the text. Don't make up your own examples. Paraphrase (restate more simply, or in fewer words) if need be.

THINK ABOUT THE WHOLE TEXT. What is this text? Who is it for? What else have you read similar to it?

The more you read; the more widely you read, the better you will cope with this Achievement Standard. See our reading list on page 160 of this book.

ISBN 9780170244220

Just one more thing ...

Achievement English @ Year 11 teaches you strategies to help you close read unfamiliar text. We have used a variety of types of both texts and questions to help you develop your own close reading skills. We have asked you to practise identifying key style features and explain how and why the author chose to use them. We have also focused on making you familiar with language terms, and their definitions, so you will be able to use them with authority as you explain what you understand about the texts.

Now that you are familiar with the more direct question there is another type of question that we would like to introduce to you. It is commonly referred to as a 'Scaffolded' Question. What is a 'scaffold'? A scaffold is a support structure, usually around a building being developed. However, when talking about a scaffolded question in English it refers to a question that offers you support, or hints, as to how to answer the question. Such a question will demand a longer, more detailed and self-structured answer.

Scaffolded questions will not ask about an isolated technique or meaning or purpose. Instead, they will ask a wider question but will give you ideas about how to answer them in depth and detail. Always use the clues.

So what does this mean?

- Instead of being given several short, specific questions you are given one or two more general questions.
- These questions demand a longer, more structured answer.
- You are often given 'hints' about what sort of information you might include in your answer.

Is that important?

- Your answer will be assessed as N, A, M, or E depending on the detail in the response you provide.
- Show that you have heeded the advice you have been given by planning your answer carefully around the hints.
- Your aim is a response that clearly expresses your understanding of the text.

Here is an example of the kind of question we are talking about:

Look at Text B as a whole.

Explain how the poet's feelings about the friendship are developed. Support your answer with examples from the text. In your answer, you could cover some of the following aspects:

- ideas
- imagery
- style
- structure
- narrative point-of-view.

Here the question gives you the overall topic of your answer and five potential points you might mention if you can find examples in the text. (If you cannot, do not use the point!)

ISBN 9780170244220

Here is a second example:

Explain how the writer shows **what the experience of the fire is like for Federico**. Support your answer with examples from the text.

You could use one or more of the following ideas as a starting point for your answer:

- the techniques, including language features, that the writer uses to show Federico's experience
- the importance of the title
- the contrast between Sylvia and Federico.

Here the question specifically invites you to use one or more of these bullet point ideas in your answer. Always try to explain the effect of any language technique you identify.

How do you tackle this kind of question? Like any other question you are asked!

You are used to answering very specific short questions relating to text. *Why is the word 'xxx' used? What does this metaphor suggest?* etc These answers are very similar, they are usually just asking you to think about the text as a whole.

As with any other question, the key thing is that you actually **answer the question**. Don't worry about the string of empty lines below the question that you feel have to fill with writing.

Use this strategy to help you:

- Read the question twice.
- Underline key words.
- Read and re-read the passage.
- Underline or highlight detail that looks important to you as you go.
- Go back to the hints or bullet points.
- Check if there's anything else in the passage you want to highlight.
- Take a few minutes to plan your answer. Think of it as a small essay.
- Make sure you are using specific language terms if possible.
- Check that you always support any point you make with an example.
- Write your answer.
- Re-read your answer – **have you answered the question?**

ISBN 9780170244220

Building an answer

A detailed answer needs just that – detail. Some students find this easier to understand in terms of points made. Here is the first verse of a poem **Little City** *by Robert Horan* about a spider.

Spider, from his flaming sleep,
staggers out into the window frame;
swings out from the red den where he slept
to nest in the gnarled glass.
Fat hero, burnished cannibal
lets down a frail ladder and ties a knot,
sways down to a landing with furry grace.

Now a question about this verse might ask what does the poet wish to draw the reader's attention to in this first verse.

A very simple answer might be

He wants the reader to notice how the spider moves.

Support for this answer might be:

He uses verbs 'staggers, swings, sways' to describe these movements.

A slightly more detailed answer might also say:

The poet also describes the spider as fat but attractively shiny and graceful in his movements.

Here's a tip – to write a detailed insightful response make sure you think about what all the important words mean – both denotation and connotation.

A more carefully constructed and detailed answer might say:

The poet wants the reader to visualise the spider emerging from a dark place, "red den" moving unsteadily at first, he 'staggers' and then more confidently, he 'swings' to a deliberate position. He will 'nest' deliberately, purposefully, set up a home for himself, against the window.

In the second part of the verse the spider is described as a "fat hero" an oxymoron, heroes are not usually fat so there is immediately some suggestion that he is not a conventional hero while suggesting he is brave and at the centre of this adventure. The spider is the described as a 'burnished cannibal' glossy, shiny but deadly to his own kind. This introduces what the spider does next: he begins to construct his web.

The writer stresses the delicacy of the spider web, using the oxymoron" a frail ladder", and describes the skilfulness of the spider as he now 'sways' and lands with 'grace'.

And a comment of more depth might also add:

There is discord in this first verse between the attractive appearance and admiration of the spider's movement and the expected inevitable outcome for other insects ,of his appearance and industry.

You might like to go over these answers and highlight the number of points the student has made. We calculate 2, 3 and 8. If you plan your answer first you can list your points and check that you've made them all at the end.

ISBN 9780170244220

Let's look at a question together

Let's look closely at a short poem written by Christina Rossetti. Read the poem carefully.

Hurt No Living Thing

Hurt no living thing;
Ladybird nor butterfly,
Nor moth with dusty wing,
Nor cricket chirping cheerily,
Nor grasshopper so light of leap,
Nor dancing gnat, nor beetle fat,
Nor harmless worms that creep.

Christina Rossetti

First ...

Find, highlight and annotate as many examples of the following as you can:

- punctuation
- nouns
- rhyme
- repetition
- alliteration
- imperative.

ISBN 9780170244220

Using your annotations above, answer the following question in as much detail as possible.

1 What is the poem's message? How is that message conveyed?

In your answer you might mention structure, vocabulary, repetition

(Use the hints to help you scaffold your response, but you can mention other techniques if you wish).

ISBN 9780170244220

On your own

Now it is time for you to have a go on your own. Below is a passage from *Adventures of Huckleberry Finn* by Mark Twain. Read the passage at least twice, annotating important features.

You don't know about me, without you have read a book by the name of "The Adventures of Tom Sawyer," but that ain't no matter. That book was made by Mr. Mark Twain, and he told the truth, mainly. There was things which he stretched, but mainly he told the truth. That is nothing.

I never seen anybody but lied, one time or another, without it was Aunt Polly¬— Tom's Aunt Polly she is—and Mary, and the Widow Douglas, is all told about in that book—which is mostly a true book; with some stretchers, as I said before.

Now the way that the book winds up, is this: Tom and me found the money that the robbers hid in the cave, and it made us rich. We got six thousand dollars apiece—all gold. It was an awful sight of money when it was piled up. Well, Judge Thatcher, he took it and put it out at interest, and it fetched us a dollar a day apiece, all the year round—more than a body could tell what to do with. The Widow Douglas, she took me for her son, and allowed she would sivilize me; but it was rough living in the house all the time, considering how dismal regular and decent the widow was in all her ways; and so when I couldn't stand it no longer I lit out. I got into my old rags, and my sugar-hogshead* again, and was free and satisfied. But Tom Sawyer, he hunted me up and said he was going to start a band of robbers and I might join if I would go back to the widow and be respectable. So I went back.

The widow she cried over me, and called me a poor lost lamb, and she called me a lot of other names, too, but she never meant no harm by it. She put me in them new clothes again, and I couldn't do nothing but sweat and sweat, and feel all cramped up. Well, then, the old thing commenced again. The widow rung a bell for supper, and you had to come to time. When you got to the table you couldn't go right to eating, but you had to wait for the widow to tuck down her head and grumble a little over the victuals, though there warn't really anything the matter with them. That is, nothing only everything was cooked by itself. In a barrel of odds and ends it is different; things get mixed up, and the juice kind of swaps around, and things go better.

After supper she got out her book and learned me abut Moses and the Bulrushers; and I was in a sweat to find out all about him; but by-and-by she let it out that Moses had been dead a considerable long time; so then I didn't care no more about him; because I don't take no stock of dead people.

Pretty soon I wanted to smoke, and asked the widow to let me. But she wouldn't. She said it was a mean practice and wasn't clean, and I must try not to do it any more. That is just the way with some people. They get down on a thing when they don't know nothing about it. Here she was bothering about Moses, which was no kin to her, and no use to anybody being gone, you see, yet finding a power of fault with me for doing a thing that had some good in it. And she took snuff too; of course that was all right, because she done it herself.

*sugar-hogshead – large barrel to hold sugar

ISBN 9780170244220

1 What is the narrative voice of this novel? What do you learn about this character in the opening paragraph?

2 What details does Paragraph 2 add to your knowledge about the narrator?

3 Looking at the passage as a whole, how does the author continue to develop your understanding of the narrator? Do not repeat anything you have already said, but you might mention:

- grammar
- sentence structure
- thoughts
- dialect words
- pronunciation
- opinions
- phrasing
- actions
- actions

4 **Extension.** How is the author commenting on society through this passage?

ISBN 9780170244220

5

Further Success

So, where do we go from here?

This section will give you further practice with Close Reading. However, as you continue to study English at school you may be asked to look for links between texts.

It can be very interesting to see things in our world from different perspectives. This kind of Close Reading asks you to look for the different viewpoints that writers bring to similar subjects and/or themes in literature and non-fiction. Rather than looking at a single text in isolation you are asked to think about how writers can look at the same subject in different ways (or how they can use different subjects to illustrate similar themes) and how they can use similar language techniques for the same or for different purposes.

In this section of the book you will begin to see how this happens.

You will use the skills you are developing to analyse a single text and widen you scope to look for ways in which text are similar to each other. This will enhance your ability to read any text with critical awareness.

Our lives are full of connections. Our literature is too.

We have chosen four texts that have links so that you can experience this type of Close Reading and we have suggested a way you might approach this type of work.

1. Read the text several times.
2. Make sure that you understand each text. Check meanings of words that you don't fully understand. Annotate the text with your meanings.
3. Think about each text separately before exploring what might link them together.

As you read look up any words you do not know. The ones highlighted in yellow are some we suggest you check that you understand.

ISBN 9780170244220

Here is the first text. It is an extract from George Forster's journal. Forster was part of James Cook's second voyage to New Zealand. This part describes landing at Astronomers Point, Dusky Sound, March 1773. (If you don't know where this is, look it up on a map.)

Text 1

Voyage Around the World

The superiority of a state of civilisation over that of barbarism could not be more clearly stated, than by the alterations and improvements we had made in this place. In the course of a few days, a small part of us had cleared away the woods from a surface of more than an acre, which fifty New Zealanders, with their tools of stone, could not have performed in three months. This spot, where immense numbers of plants left to themselves lived and decayed by turn, in one confused inanimated heap; this spot, we had converted into an active scene, where a hundred and twenty men pursued various branches of employment with unremitting ardour.

...

We felled tall timber-trees, which, but for ourselves, had crumbled to dust with age; our sawyers cut them into planks, or we split them into billets for fuel. By the side of a murmuring rivulet, whose passage into the sea we facilitated, a long range of casks, which had been prepared by our coopers for that purpose, stood ready to be filled with water. Here ascended the steam of a large cauldron, in which we brewed, from neglected indigenous plants, a salutary and palatable potion, for the use of our labourers. In the offing, some of our crew appeared providing a meal of delicious fish for the refreshment of their fellows

...

But this pleasing picture of improvement was not to last, and like a meteor, vanished as suddenly as it was formed. We re-imbarked all our instruments and utensils, and left no other vestiges of our residence, than a piece of ground, from whence we had cleared the wood. We sowed indeed a quantity of European garden seeds of the best kinds; but it is obvious that the shoots of the surrounding weeds will shortly stifle every salutary and useful plant, and that in a few years our abode no longer discernible, must return to its original chaotic state.

What do these words suggest?

Find other personal pronouns in the passage. Why does the writer use them?

What does this phrase suggest?

What does this phrase want to suggest to the readers?

Find other action verbs. Why are they chosen?

What does this word suggest?

What sort of potion are they making? Why?

What figure of speech is this? What does it suggest?

Contrast the seeds and the weeds. Does the writer contradict himself?

What does this phrase suggest?

ISBN 9780170244220

Firstly answer the questions annotated around the text. The questions are designed to help you think in some depth about what the passage is saying and how it is written. Write on the book if it is yours. If it is not, answer on your own paper.

Now think about the passage as a whole. Fill in this grid to help you gather your thoughts.

What is it **about**?	Who is the **audience**?	What is the **style**?	What is the **purpose**?
	You may need to do some research.		

Make notes on:

What the sailors did to the land that altered and improved the land when they arrived. And why.

What Forster thought of the local place and people.

What Forster admires.

What Forster regrets.

ISBN 9780170244220

The second text is also an extract. This time it is from *Cook's Sites. Revisiting History* by Nicholas Thomas and Mark Adams. They comment on Forster's words when they visit Astronomers Point over two hundred years later.

Again, check the meaning of any unfamiliar words in the passage and read it several times to help your understanding of its meaning.

Text 2

The words 'then' and 'now' – comment on how the writer has placed them in the sentence and how they integrate with the simile used in the same sentence.

…

At Astronomers Point we are close to the events of 1773 for another reason, because Forster was wrong about the local ecological impact. The low hill that forms the point has not 'returned to its original chaotic state'. Forster could not have known how slowly trees decayed and grew in this temperate forest, which is further south than Tasmania, as far south as Patagonia. The stumps of some of those then felled can be discerned now, like obscure monuments shrouded in kidney fern.

…

Forster supposed that the cleared area would degenerate again into chaos, but the disorder that strikes us now is not a primeval condition but the upshot of contact. It figures not as a marker of a lack of civilisation, but as historical evidence for the beginnings of civilisation, as an organic monument to first efforts to deforest this area, and the first European efforts to deforest any part of New Zealand.

Forster's ready identification of clearing trees with civilising reaches us awkwardly, in fact simply badly. While he could associate the removal of vegetation with honest labour … we are accustomed to regard the destruction of trees as vandalism in the name of progress, and indeed as ultimately life-threatening, via the destruction of the ozone layer and the greenhouse effect.

What do these phrases suggest about the writer's attitude towards Forster?

'…the upshot of contact…' Explain what the writer is saying here.

What is the difference between Forster's view of tree felling and the writer's?

Firstly answer the questions annotated around the text. The questions are designed to help you think in some depth about what the passage is saying and how it is written. Write on the book if it is yours. If it is not, answer on your own paper.

Now think about the passage as a whole. Fill in this grid to help you gather your thoughts.

What is the text **about**?	Who is the **audience**?	What is its **style**?	What is its **purpose**?

It is relatively straightforward to see how this text relates to Text 1. Think also about how it has links with the other two texts after you have read and thought about them.

ISBN 9780170244220

Text 3

Who is the 'we' in the title?

'tongue-stump' and 'bandage' are emotive words. What do they suggest to you?

The third section of the poem moves on to 'deep time'. What has happened?

The Mess We Made at Port Chalmers

Tongue-stump of headland bandaged with concrete,
Obliterated beaches stacked with chopsticks.

All of this takes place in shallow time.

In deep time, the trees have already recovered the hills
and the machines rust, immobile, flaking away.
Healing, the land has shifted in its sleep.

All we would see if we were here
is seed-pods moving on the water.

Cilla McQueen, 1994

'stacked with chopsticks' is a figure of speech. Explain why it has been used. What does 'obliterated' mean?

What do you understand by 'deep' and 'shallow' time?

What do the final two lines suggest to you?

Extension:

You may wish to do a little research to find out what Port Chalmers looks like if you do not live in the area. It ALWAYS helps to know what you are reading about! Here's one clue for an internet seach: 'Dark Matter, Hotere and Language'.

Also you might look at the structure of the poem. Check where the sentences end. Look at the verse structure and how it links to meaning.

As you read the poem a few times answer the questions annotated around the text. The questions are designed to help you think in some depth about what the poem is saying and how it is written. Write on the book if it is yours. If it is not, answer on your own paper.

Now think about the poem as a whole. Fill in this grid to help you gather your thoughts.

What is the text **about**?	Who is the **audience**?	What is its **style**?	What is its **purpose**?
	Research may be needed.		

How does this poem link to the other texts? Jot down any thoughts you might have.

ISBN 9780170244220

Text 4

This text is an extract from an article on the Forest and Bird website.

This adjective is placed in contrast to what? And why?

What do these nouns tell you about the writer?

Waitangi Week End Trip to Western Southland and the South Coast

Sixteen people met at Outautau on a fine clear morning on Waitangi Day to explore the forests and coast of Southland. Our first foray was a 4W drive trip to Bald Hill on the top of the Long wood Range. The first part of the trip until we reached the Porakino River was through a production forest of fir and pine, after which we climbed up through pure Southland Beech and its associated under storey. Lunch was at the quarry near the locked gate. After which it was a pleasant walk to the top to wander through the mixed tussock, kanuka, flax and dracophyllum environment. Celmisia were still in flower and the gentians were starting to do so. The views of Southland were extensive.

Next morning after spending the night in Tuatapere we drove to the Alton Burn and through the Rowellen Forest to the LillBurn This forest was a mixed Southland beech/ podocarp forest that was milled some 50-60 years ago. The then New Zealand Forest Service required that a few adult beech trees per hectare be left as seed trees after the felling. This was successful, and now we see a dense, mostly beech, forest regenerating. The under storey of totara, miro, lancewood and horopito are also making strong but slower growth. While the original felling of the forest upset the whole ecology of the forest it was interesting to see how nature exerts itself given time. Stops were made to photograph patches of mistletoe which were in full flower.

How do these words link to Texts 1 and 2?

Lunch we had at Lake Hauaoko in the mixed podocarp/ mountain beech forest at the end of the road.

On our return down the Lillburn valley we turned off left to visit the remains of the Dean Forest, and paid a visit to the Big Totara Reserve managed by DoC. Here the many podocarps were impressive, especially so the few old totaras that escaped the axe and saw. Some of the large totaras, one reputed to be over a thousand years old, were awe-inspiring. May they be left in peace.

Compare this with the sentiment expressed in paragraph 1 of Text 1.

Comment on the use of emotive words like these in the passage.

ISBN 9780170244220

Now think about the text as a whole. Fill in this grid to help you gather your thoughts.

What is the text **about**?	Who is the **audience**?	What is its **style**?	What is its **purpose**?

How does this text link to the other texts? Jot down any thought you might have.

Making connections

Having studied each text independently, it is time to look across the texts. Answer these questions in your own words, using reference to at least two texts to support your ideas in each answer:

You might use the grids you have filled in to help you form a basis for your answers using the similarities and differences in:

- *Content: the subject of each text.*
- *Audience: for whom the writer is writing.*
- *Style: vocabulary, nouns and verbs; descriptive words like adjectives and adverbs; figures of speech; facts; emotive words...*
- *Purpose: theme/s, ideas, opinions, intentions...*

1. What connections in time and place can you see in these texts?

2. Describe any similar theme or themes in at least two texts.

ISBN 9780170244220

3. Do any of the writers have similar opinions?
Do any of these writers have different opinions?

On your own ... again

Now that you have worked through our example it is time for you to have a go on your own. Remember to apply everything you have learnt in the previous sections.

Carefully read the instructions so you are aware of exactly what you need to do.

Take each text in turn and:

- Read it through once for understanding
- Read it through again circling, underlining, linking ideas etc as you go.
- Look at any specific questions on the text and answer them.

There is a question that requires you to read 'across the text', ie, pull information from several texts. You will need to:

- Read the question several times to ensure you understand what is being asked.
- Go back to each text and skim read until you get to a place that has relevant information.
- Read this part (and a little before and a little after).
- Stop and think about how this connects to the other passages. Jot any ideas you have on the side of the text.
- Do the same for each passage. However be aware that you don't necessarily need to use information from all the texts, perhaps just two are sufficient to that question.
- Using the notes you have jotted down form an answer to the question in the space provided, making sure that you clearly reference the text and draw conclusions in your answer.

ISBN 9780170244220

Text 1

This passage is an extract from a novel written in 1908. Read the passage at least twice and look up the highlighted words to help you understand the passage well. Answer the questions that follow in as much detail as possible.

From *The Old Wives' Tale*

Constance had returned to the window, her expectancy apparently unappeased.

"I don't like the look of that cloud," she murmured.

"What! Are they out still?" Samuel inquired, taking off his overcoat.

"Here they are!" cried Constance. Her features suddenly transfigured, she sprang to the door, pulled it open, and descended the steps.

A perambulator was being rapidly pushed up the slope by a breathless girl.

"Amy," Constance gently protested, "I told you not to venture far."

"I hurried all I could, mum, soon as I seed that cloud," the girl puffed, with the air of one who is seriously thankful to have escaped a great disaster.

Constance dived into the recesses of the perambulator and extricated from its cocoon the centre of the universe, and scrutinized him with quiet passion, and then rushed with him into the house though not a drop or rain had yet fallen.

"Precious!" exclaimed Amy, in ecstasy, her young virginal eyes following him til he disappeared. Then she wheeled away the perambulator, which now had no more value nor interest than an eggshell. It was necessary to take it right round to the Brougham Street yard entrance, past the front door of the closed shop.

Constance sat down on the horsehair sofa and hugged and kissed her prize before removing his bonnet.

by Arnold Bennett

1 Who appears in this passage?

2 Describe Constance's behaviour in the first four sentences of the passage.

3 How does the writer use hyperbole and metaphor to suggest that this child is extremely important in the lives of the three adults?

ISBN 9780170244220

Text 2

This is an extract from a graphic novel. Billy, a fifteen year old who has a new interest in falconry, is at home on a Saturday night with his mother.

Read the text at least twice and look up any words you don't understand. Answer the question that follows in as much detail as possible.

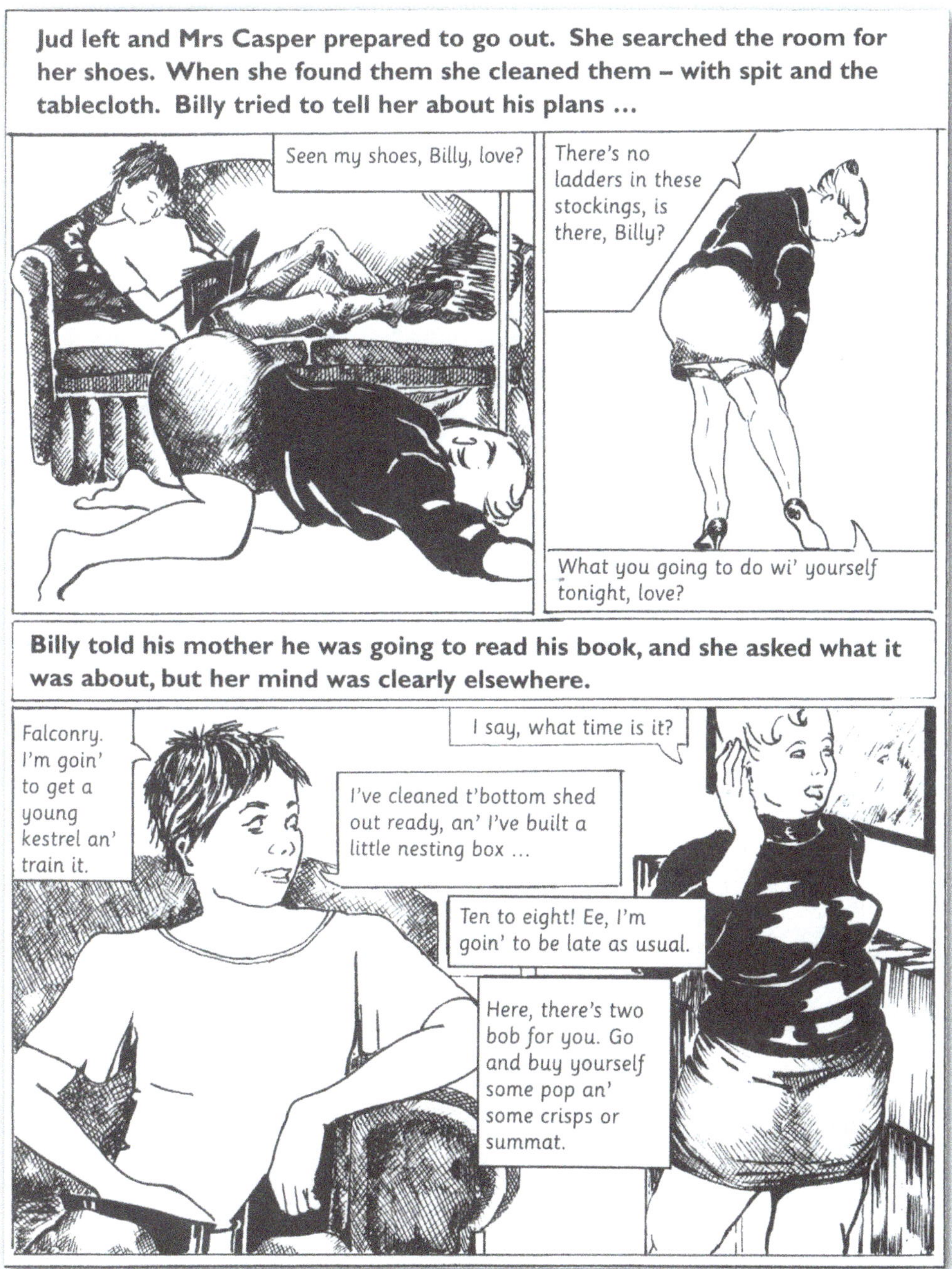

1 How do the writer *and* the illustrator show that this mother is imperfect?

Text 3

This passage is an extract from an autobiography written in 2003. Read the passage at least twice and look up the highlighted words to help you understand the passage well. Answer the questions that follow in as much detail as possible.

From *Travels with my Mother*

The author is remembering a time in his childhood when he was bullied on his way home from school.

Then suddenly they are there as if they always have been, materialised by my arrival in their malevolent force field. I pull up, defeated. They are tall, neatly turned out and they wear dress gloves like grown-ups wear.

One is blonde, with ponytails swaying from beneath her maroon bonnet; the other, dark-eyed, has a cruel face and a hooked nose, which, it absurdly occurs to me, might peck my eyes out. They circle on their bikes, far enough away to be able to change direction suddenly if I fancy I see an escape route and make to break...

Every so often one swoops and swipes at me, or pinches or grabs a flap of ear roughly between her gloved thumb and fingertip. One flicks the baby blue sunhat with its foreign legion neck flap from my head and it lies on the road; the other rides back and forth over it leaving grubby streaks of tyre and dirt.

"Ooooh, look!" cries one. "Now his hat's dirty. Mummy won't be happy."

"Who's a very bad boy?" says the other.

As they circle they keep up the talk, filling the silence with threatening noise. Their chant is a tormentors' duet, sneering and discordant, a round song in which one always starts before the other finishes. I freeze in the dust and fight back tears. Mostly I don't want to cry because they are girls.

...

Consumed by their taunting presence, I don't notice the car skid to a halt. The avenger is among them before I realise what is happening. It's the car I see first, the elegant sweeping lines of the silver-grey and navy two-tone Daimler Conquest. Its door is open and I can see the walnut dashboard and the blue leather upholstery.

With a start of recognition, I realise it's our car and I turn my attention to the two girls. Mum has dragged then from their bicycles (which topple with an agreeable solid clank) and has them in hand, rough knots of maroon blazer in each clenched fist. From time to time, she lets one go for an instant so she can cuff the other across the side of the head with a free hand. But mostly she just holds on and they don't even struggle to get away.

ISBN 9780170244220

She is bellowing at them and they cower as she shakes them, promising that they will get "what for" if they don't leave me alone. They seem to regard this as a disagreeable proposition. They have no idea what "what for" is, though they reason, soundly enough, that it's a good deal worse than being dragged from your bike and marauded by an angry mother. I notice as they remount and pedal away panic-stricken that their ties are skewed and that old Hook Nose clutches her bonnet, which is crushed by her grip on the handlebars.

Sniffling, I pull myself together as Mum picks up my hat and dusts it off and I clamber into the car's cool interior and collapse against the soft leather of the seat. I ride home in splendour.

A few weeks later, I see the girls for the last time. They are in the distance, riding with a kind of slow, stately dignity, their stockinged knees rising and falling, when they catch sight of me. The effect is electric. The balance of their riding becomes suddenly wobbly and uncertain. One turns hard left onto the verge and the other makes a messy U and begins pedalling back the way she came. Then, after what must have been a brief consultation, they disappear down a public path that leads to the state housing subdivision on the other side of the road.

Peter Calder

1 How can you tell that this event happened quite a long time ago?

2 How does the writer show that the girls are bullies?

3 Who is the avenger? What is an avenger? Is this hyperbole?

4 What is the importance of the hats?

Text 4

Read the poem at least twice. Read it aloud if appropriate. Look up any words you do not understand. Answer the questions that follow in as much detail as possible.

Dress Sense

You're not going out in that, are you?
I've never seen anything
More ridiculous in my whole life.
You look like you've been dragged
Through a hedge backwards
And lost half your dress along the way.

What's wrong with it?
You're asking me what's wrong with that?
Everything: that's what. It's loud, it's common,
It reveals far too much of your ...
Your ... well your 'what you shouldn't be revealing'.

No, I'm not going to explain;
You know very well what I mean, young lady
But you choose to ignore
Every single piece of reasonable helpful advice
That you are offered.

It's not just the neckline I'm talking about
- And you can hardly describe it as a neckline,
More like a navel-line
If you bother to observe the way that it plunges.
Have you taken a look at the back?
(What little there is of it.)
Have you?

Boys are only going to think
One thing
When they see you in that outfit.
Where on earth did you get it?
And don't tell me that my money paid for it
Whatever you do.

You found it where?

Well, it probably looked different on her
And, anyway, you shouldn't be going through
Your mother's old clothes.

David Kitchen

ISBN 9780170244220

1 Who is the speaker in this poem?

2 Comment on the structure of the poem. What is missing?

3 What does the father criticise about the dress? And why?

4 Comment on the use of hyperbole, and simile in the poem

An aside on ... compare and contrast

The word 'compare' means to examine people or things to look for **similarities**.
The word 'contrast' means to look for **differences**.

Usually you will be asked to find similarities between texts, you will be asked to compare them. The texts may have similar subject matter, similar themes, or similar styles.

You may also notice contrasts between the text and a strong student will be able to comment on the differences too.

ISBN 9780170244220

Making connections

Now try to find links between these passages.

1 Using at least TWO of these passages answer this question in as much detail as you can.

Here are some clues to help you out. What links can you see between these text?
Think about:

Subject matter	What are the text about? Common ideas?
Writer/Narrator	Is the writer the narrator? Different voices, different opinions?
Figurative language	Look at hyberbole, simile, metaphor in particular. Do the authors use these in similar ways?
Tone	Think about the differences in tones of voices.
Themes	What messages are being conveyed? Differences? Similarities?

ISBN 9780170244220

Understanding Text – the Essay

6

In the study of English at Year 11 you will be asked to answer questions on a variety of text, both in the classroom and under examination conditions. The word *text* is used to mean any written or visual piece.

You will need to answer ONE from each of these categories...

Written text	
novel	short story
non-fiction	poetry
drama script	print media

Visual/oral text	
film	drama production
television programme	song lyric
radio programme	multimedia text
graphic novel	

This question will focus on one of the following:

1 Theme

What are the main ideas that the author/director wants us to think about?

2 Character

Major: Who is/are the main character/s? What are they like as human beings? How does the author/director reveal their character to us? By their actions? Their speech? By what others say about them? By the language used to describe them? Do the characters change in the course of the work?

Minor: These are important characters too. Why has the author included them? To allow for a subplot? As a contrast to the major characters? To interact with the major characters?

3 Setting

Time, place, social background. How does this affect the characters and/or theme?

4 Audience

Who is this text created for? How can you tell?

5 Personal response

What do you think of the work? Its characters, ideas? Is there any relevance to your world?

6 Style

The way a piece has been written. What features of style has the author/director used and why.

7 Techniques

If your text is visual how do:

- verbal techniques (soundtrack, music etc)
- visual techniques (camera angles, lighting, costume, makeup, special effects)

contribute to your understanding of the text?

If your text is a poem you may need to focus on language techniques like figures of speech, emotive words etc.

ISBN 9780170244220

Before you go any further ...

In this section of the course you will need to write at least one essay on a variety of text. The essay will need to be at least 200 words in a formal style. It is important that you practise the necessary skills, as once you can write a successful essay on one text you can apply what you have learnt about style and structure to any further essays.

Every year, after the external assessments, the Examiners write a report for teachers. Every year they say pretty much the same things. Let's remind you of some of their helpful comments regarding writing literary essays. Although we are sure your teacher tells you these things, often!

- *... refrain from presenting only a plot summary ...*

Translation

- Do not just retell the story of the text you have studied. Your examiner already knows the plot, probably better than you do.

- *... select topics carefully to ensure [you] can deal with the demands of the topic before beginning ... take note of the key words in bold to guide [your] answers.*

Translation

- Choose a question that you know the answer to. Then answer that question!

- *... keep to the topic ... avoid trying to use rote-learned essays from previous years' papers ...*

Translation

- Do your own work – both the thinking and the writing.

- *... support [your] ideas with appropriate evidence / examples from the text ... provide sufficient evidence to enable [you] to achieve the standard, using the suggested minimum word length as a guide.*

Translation

- Always use references to and quotations from the text. Write more than the minimum number of words required.

- *... proof-read [your] answers, ... Some candidates' punctuation let them down. Candidates also included detailed examples as 'add ons' using only commas, resulting in rambling 'run on' sentences. There was also a tendency to use conjunctions to amplify ideas, which resulted in long, grammatically incorrect sentences.*

Translation

- Write as accurately as possible. (We include all this detail to convince you that *how* you write is as important as what you say. In fact, the two are undeniably linked).

The following examples show different ways in which students have written successful essays on text. Work through each example applying the suggestions to your own work.

ISBN 9780170244220

How to write a text essay on character

Describe a challenge faced by a character in the text. Explain how the challenge helped you understand an idea (or ideas) in the text.

Look for the key words

Describe a **challenge** faced by a character in the text. Explain **how** the challenge helped you **understand an idea (or ideas)** in the text.

Even short questions need to be carefully unpacked so that you answer the question fully. In this question, the word 'challenge' can lead students astray. Remember, a challenge is not always physical. It might be to do with emotions or relationships.

Structuring your essay

This essay will need *at least* two paragraphs to cover the description of the challenge and the explanation of how the challenge helped you understand the idea. Ideally you would have two explanations of how the challenge supported the theme.

FINDING THE APPROPRIATE CONTENT

To start with you will need to read through all the notes you have on character and theme. This will refresh you memory with what you have studied. It is likely you will choose one of the main characters of your text but you will need to spend some time choosing the appropriate 'challenge'. If the challenge does not clearly connect to a theme you will have difficulty trying to pull the loose links between the two into an essay.

Here are the notes that the student copied down from the whiteboard before she began planning this essay.

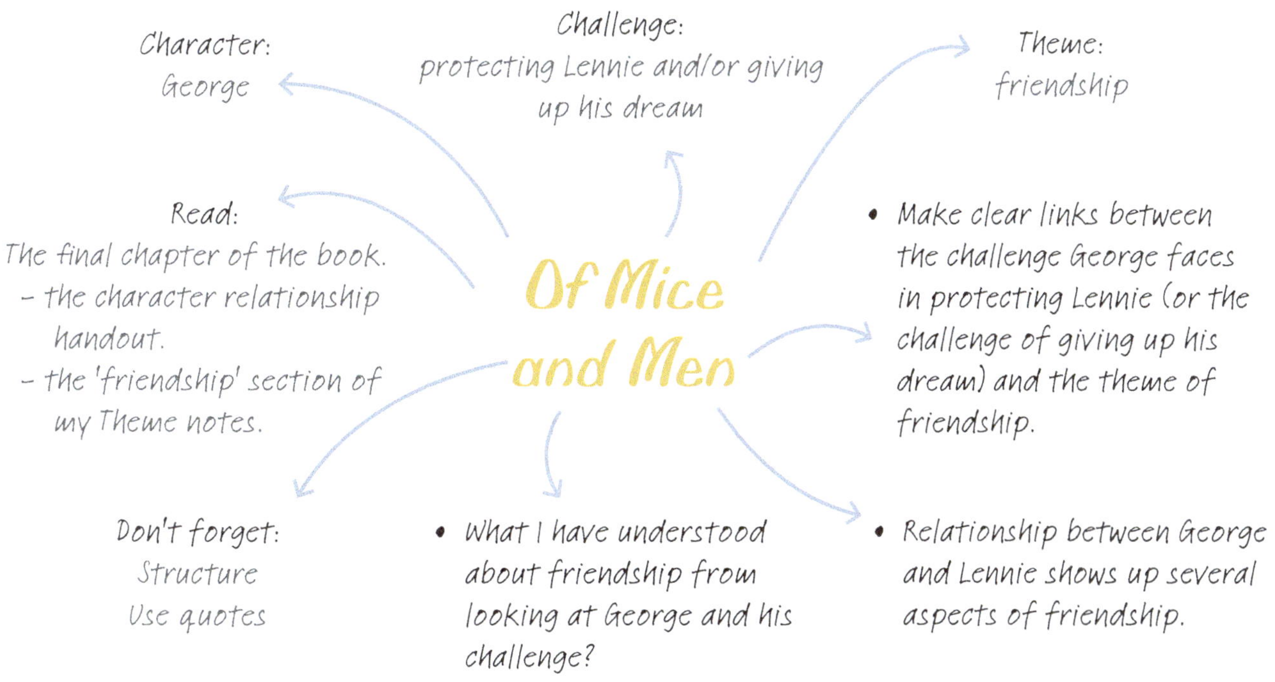

Of Mice and Men

Character:
George

Challenge:
protecting Lennie and/or giving up his dream

Theme:
friendship

Read:
The final chapter of the book.
- the character relationship handout.
- the 'friendship' section of my Theme notes.

- Make clear links between the challenge George faces in protecting Lennie (or the challenge of giving up his dream) and the theme of friendship.

Don't forget:
Structure
Use quotes

- What I have understood about friendship from looking at George and his challenge?

- Relationship between George and Lennie shows up several aspects of friendship.

ISBN 9780170244220

Crafting your work

Now look at how the student crafted an essay with the information selected.

George Milton is one of the two main characters in the novel Of Mice and Men by John Steinbeck. He faces the challenge of protecting his best friend and this challenge has shown me that true friendship can be a difficult burden, which is a theme of this novel.

George and his mate Lennie Small are two adult men who are wandering across America in search of farm work. George seems to be the older of the two and he is the one who looks after Lennie, who is a bit simple. George and Lennie have a dream that they will save up some money and live 'off the fatta the lan'' with their own 'little house and a couple of acres'.

Unfortunately Lennie gets into trouble at the farm where they are working. He likes to pet soft things like rabbits but he tries to 'pat' the boss's son's wife who has flirted with him. She screams in fear and he kills her accidentally because he is incredibly strong.

The challenge for George is that he must accept that their plan will not be possible now and he must work out how best to be Lennie's friend. Should he just accept that Lennie has done wrong and must be punished? He was getting fed up with looking after Lennie, keeping him out of trouble and threatened to leave him behind often. But in reality he loves Lennie, Lennie is his only friend and they support each other. He wants to help Lennie escape because he knows the woman's death wasn't really Lennie's fault. He wants to protect Lennie from the other cowboys because he knows they will kill Lennie in a horrible way if they can catch him.

George finds Lennie down by the river and they talk about their plans again, how they will buy a farm and be happy together living the simple life. As he talks and build this picture in Lennie's head George puts a gun to Lennie's temple and shoots him. In this way he protects his friend and prevents him from being hurt by others. He faces the challenge that to protect his best friend he has to end that friend's life but in the kindest way he can.

The idea in this text that I can understand is that true friendship is not easy. George has a dreadful challenge to face because he cannot help Lennie to escape so he has to end his best friend's life in the kindest way he can to protect him from a worse fate. George wanted to be 'somebody' and by carrying out this act he is somebody, he is a true friend to Lennie. It is a high price to pay as he has lost his only friend and his dream of a better life, too. The challenge he faced shows clearly the theme of friendship in this novel, the theme that friendship is not an easy thing to offer or to remain true to.

Note that the first time each character is mentioned the student uses their full name.

This student identifies the challenge they are going to write about right at the beginning. They also clearly state what theme they will connect it to.

The student spends time describing the relationship between George and Lennie. In this case it helps explain how Lennie was a burden to George. Use detail from the plot only if it is directly relevant to your point.

Key words from the question are used to help keep the essay focused.

Notice how the student uses the key word 'challenge' to link this part of the topic and to demonstrate their awareness of how the character 'faces' that challenge.

The student clearly explains how the character has helped them understand the theme. It is an important part of the question and must be answered.

The student sums up the essay in their final sentence. This sentence could have stood alone as a final paragraph.

DIY (DO IT YOURSELF!)

Now plan an essay that responds to the same topic using a text that you have studied. Aim to write a 250-350 word essay, making sure that you include reference to the text and suitable quotations.

ISBN 9780170244220

How to write a text essay on character relationship and change

Describe a relationship and explain how and why it changed.

Look for the key words

Describe a **relationship** and **explain how** and **why** it **changed**.

Even short questions need to be carefully unpacked so that you answer the question fully. In this question, the word 'relationship' can lead students astray. Remember a relationship is not necessarily a love interest. It might be a friendship, a business partnership, a family link or even a negative relationship like leaders of opposing gangs, and so on.

Structuring your essay

This essay will need at least three paragraphs to cover the relationship at the beginning of the text, the changes that occur and the reasons for those changes.

FINDING THE APPROPRIATE CONTENT

Read through all the notes in your folder on characters and their relationships. Select a relationship that does change and prepare an outline for your essay giving detail that clearly shows features of the relationship that change and the reasons why.

Below is an example of how a student has organised information for an essay based on Laurie Saunders and Amy Smith in the novel *The Wave* by Morten Rhue.

Relationships in *The Wave*

AMY & LAURIE

WHAT THE RELATIONSHIP WAS LIKE AT THE BEGINNING OF THE STORY:

- 'best friends' did practically everything together
- ate their lunch together
- both 'straight A' students
- both upset by the film shown in History class
- hang out together
  - went to the football every Saturday together
  - Amy often spent time with Laurie in the Grapevine office
- sense of humour, e.g. Gabondi's French class
- even though they were best friends, that constant competition somehow prevented them from being really close.

THINGS THAT HAPPENED TO SHOW A DIFFERENCE:

- argued
- limited contact – first time in 3 years they didn't sit together at the football
- argument in the library
- 'Laurie, you are not a princess any more'.

WHY THE RELATIONSHIP CHANGED:

- the end to the friendship came as a result of The Wave
- Amy firmly for The Wave
- Laurie anti The Wave
- Amy liked the idea that everyone was equal
- 'For the first time in 3 years I don't have to keep up with Laurie Saunders any more.'

ISBN 9780170244220

Crafting your work

Now look at how the student crafted an essay with the information selected.

Use characters' full names for the first time you use them in an essay.

This student has incorporated the introduction (and conclusion) into the essay.

During the novel The Wave by Morten Rhue an important relationship was between Laurie Saunders and Amy Smith who were best friends. They did practically everything together. They ate their lunch at school together, they went to football every Saturday and often spent time hanging out in Laurie's Grapevine office. Laurie and Amy shared a similar sense of humour. This was shown in the 'fish face' incident in the French class. They were both straight A students and were both upset by the film on Nazi Germany that Mr Ross showed them in History.

Note that only information with direct relevance to the question is used in these paragraphs.

As The Wave became more active Laurie and Amy's relationship began to deteriorate. Not only did they disagree on The Wave but they saw less and less of each other, no longer did they spend time together at school or go to the football. 'Suddenly it was as if she was a stranger.' Now whenever they met they argued about The Wave and this meant that there was no pleasure in the friendship any more. When Laurie told Amy that she was going to print an article against The Wave they argued. Amy says 'the only reason you're against The Wave is because it means you're not a princess any more'.

Look carefully at how you use quotations. Make sure you let the quotations support your point rather than repeat what you've already said.

Laurie and Amy's change of relationship came about as a direct result of The Wave. Laurie was firmly anti The Wave while Amy was as firmly for it. Amy liked The Wave because she felt it made everyone equal. She told Laurie '... it means that nobody is better than anyone else for once'. However Laurie sees the negative effects of The Wave on the students in the school and she is determined to fight against it even though it might cost her the friendship of her best friend Amy.

This student uses three clear paragraphs to answer the question. One on before, one on after, one on why. Structuring your essay like this ensures you answer all aspects of the question. Note: the 'why' paragraph could also be inserted between the before and after.

DIY (DO IT YOURSELF!)

Now plan an essay that responds to the same topic using a text that you have studied. Aim to write a 250-350 word essay, making sure that you include reference to the text and suitable quotations.

ISBN 9780170244220

How to write a text essay on setting

Describe a setting and the effect it had on the story.

Note: There are very few texts that can be used to answer a setting question effectively. Unless you have detailed notes on setting and your teacher has indicated that a setting question is an option for your text DO NOT answer it!

Finding the key words

Describe a **setting** and the **effect** it had on the story.

The word *effect* invites you to talk about the way the *setting* is important to the story. Does it influence a character to act, think and react in a certain way? Understand a point of view offered from another character? Does it help the reader to understand what living in that time/place/social background is like? Some text may have more than one setting. Note that this question asks you to write about just **one** setting.

Structuring your essay

When you plan your essay make sure that you have at least one detailed paragraph about the effect of the setting or enough information to make a comment about effect in each paragraph that describes the setting.

FINDING THE APPROPRIATE CONTENT

You will need to describe the setting accurately, including specific detail and quotations from the text, but you must be careful not to let your essay be dominated by description. In the following plan, based on the setting of Hell from *Tomorrow, When the War Began* by John Marsden, you can see that the student has begun with a physical description but has three significant effects to use in the essay.

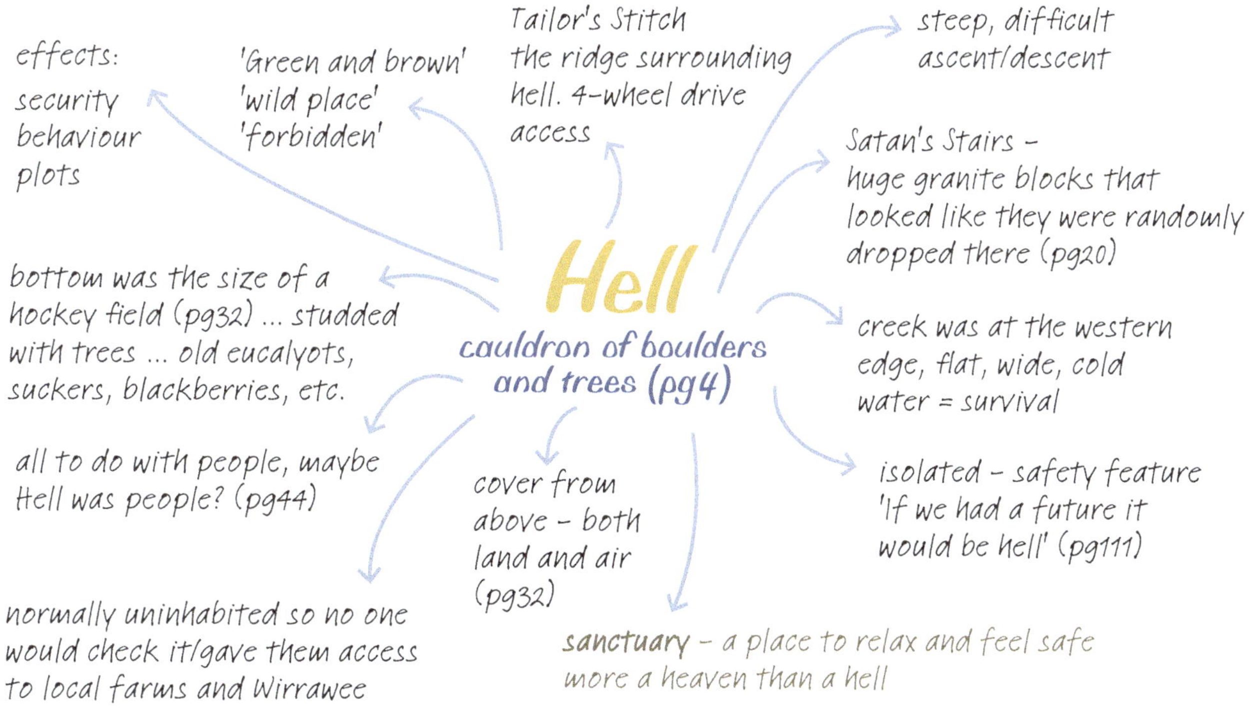

Hell
cauldron of boulders and trees (pg4)

effects:
security
behaviour
plots

'Green and brown'
'wild place'
'forbidden'

Tailor's Stitch
the ridge surrounding hell. 4-wheel drive access

steep, difficult ascent/descent

Satan's Stairs – huge granite blocks that looked like they were randomly dropped there (pg20)

bottom was the size of a hockey field (pg32) ... studded with trees ... old eucalyots, suckers, blackberries, etc.

creek was at the western edge, flat, wide, cold water = survival

all to do with people, maybe Hell was people? (pg44)

cover from above – both land and air (pg32)

isolated – safety feature 'If we had a future it would be hell' (pg111)

normally uninhabited so no one would check it/gave them access to local farms and Wirrawee

sanctuary – a place to relax and feel safe more a heaven than a hell

ISBN 9780170244220

Crafting your essay

Now look at how the student crafted an essay with the information selected.

This year I studied Tomorrow, When the War Began by John Marsden. An important setting in the book is 'Hell'. Hell was the main setting for the novel and was important because for Ellie and her friends it was their sanctuary from the people who had invaded Australia and captured their families.

The setting of Hell was a kaleidoscope of 'green and brown'. It is a 'wild place', a cauldron of boulders, trees, blackberries and undergrowth. It has spectacular cliffs, some called 'Satan's Steps', leading down into it. Satan's Steps are 'huge granite blocks'. Hell had a small creek running through and this supplied them with water. The soil in Hell would have been of high quality because the group planned to grow vegetables for food.

Ellie and her friends gained access to Hell the hard way, down 'Satan's Steps'. Because it was so difficult to access it meant that they were safe from the enemy when they were in Hell. At the bottom there was a large flat basin about the 'size of the hockey field'. This was dotted with trees which provided shelter.

Hell was where the group had been camping when the invasion began and they continued to meet there after they had been out into the town of Wirrawee. The group travelled into Wirrawee for supplies and information of how their families were. Hell was their sanctuary, a place they could relax and feel safe. It had all they needed to survive and they thought in advance to improve Hell for the long run.

The setting had an important effect on the story because despite the name they originally gave it, Hell helped them to survive. The effect of the setting was that they were safe from the enemy who could see no access into the area and could not see the camp-site from the air because of the cover the trees and bush provided. Also because it was normally an uninhabited part of the district the soldiers would not think anyone could live there and therefore not search the area. The teenagers could also make raids into Wirrawee and the surrounding farms for supplies without detection.

The essay question asked for only one setting. Notice how this essay focuses solely on Hell, not Wirrawee, and so on.

This student has used quotations well. Instead of leaving them 'hanging' at the end of a sentence the quotations have been incorporated into a sentence.

Note the detail found in these paragraphs. You must provide detail in order to score well.

Questions on setting may be phrased in different ways:

- Explain, with detailed reasons, how the setting of your text affected the characters or events.
- Describe the setting of the story and explain why it was important.
- Explain how the place and/or time your text is set in is important.

However they all require very similar information. Always read the key words carefully and adapt your information to suit.

Although there is a paragraph that explains the effect of the setting there are also 'implied' reasons throughout the first three paragraphs, for example, 'Hell was their sanctuary, a place they could relax and feel safe'. Use a highlighter to mark other implied effects mentioned.

DIY (DO IT YOURSELF!)

Now plan an essay that responds to the same topic using a text that you have studied. Aim to write a 250-350 word essay, making sure that you describe the setting accurately including specific detail and quotations from the text.

ISBN 9780170244220

How to write a text essay on the opening scene

Briefly describe the opening scene of your text and explain how effective it is.

Finding the key words

Briefly describe the **opening** scene of your text and **explain** how **effective** it is.

The *opening* could refer to the first scene of a film, the first act of a play, the first chapter of a novel or the first paragraph of a short story. You must use your judgement to decide if your text has enough in the opening scene to warrant attempting a question of this type.

Structuring your essay

The word *briefly* must be noted. Explaining the *effectiveness* should be the most important part of this essay. It is possible to intertwine the description and the effectiveness rather than separate them into distinct paragraphs.

FINDING THE APPROPRIATE CONTENT

Re-read (or view or listen to) the opening scene carefully. Think about how these first introductions and events relate to the rest of the text. Some ideas you could think about are:

- Does it start with an exciting or suspenseful event?
- Does it start at a moment of conflict?
- Does it present a question that makes you want to read on?
- Does it create an interesting atmosphere?
- Does it introduce character/s?
- Does it suggest the main theme?
- Does it provide details of background, time or place?

Here is a student's plan for an essay based on Act 1, Scene 1 of Shakespeare's *Romeo and Juliet*.

WHAT HAPPENS?	EFFECT?
Fight scene between servants that starts over nothing. Benvolio and Tybalt join in.	Exciting for audience, grabs attention. Shows pettiness. Tells us there is a feud happening and affecting everyone (the whole city). Introduces characters, Benvolio not so keen to fight – Tybalt fiery.
Montague and Capulet arrive. Prince Escalus breaks it up and warns the Capulets and Montagues never to fight in public again.	They want to fight too. Sets up a tension.
Lovesick Romeo enters.	Introduction of main character. Not interested in fighting.

ISBN 9780170244220

Crafting your writing

Now look at how the same student crafted an essay with the information selected.

The play Romeo and Juliet by William Shakespeare opens first with the Prologue which tells in a fourteen line sonnet the story of the play and how it will end in tragedy for 'two star-crossed lovers'. The action then begins with a fight scene on the streets of Verona between the servants of the house of Montague, Sampson and Gregory, and a man of the house of Capulet, Abraham. Others including Tybalt, a Capulet relation, and Benvolio, a Montague friend, join in and the whole town is affected by the rioting. Even the elderly heads of the families want to be involved. The fighting does not stop until the Prince commands them to stop and threatens exile on anyone breaking the peace.

This opening is effective because it immediately grabs the attention of the audience with its dramatic action and movements and it introduces several significant characters like Tybalt and Benvolio. It is also effective because the audience is able to see how petty the feud is, it begins with Abraham accusing Sampson of 'biting his thumb' at him. Also we see how all-embracing the feud is when Tybalt says, 'What drawn and talk of peace? I hate the word as I hate Hell, all Montagues and thee'. Everyone from the fathers to the servants is involved. We also learn how long-standing the feud is, the town is used to the fighting and it takes the Prince himself to stop it. This is effective because it prepares us for the difficulties Romeo and Juliet will face.

The opening scene is also effective because it introduces one of the two main characters, Romeo, the son of the house of Capulet, who is the only one not interested in fighting. He is in love.

All the main ideas of the play are begun in this first scene: the feud that prevents the lovers being together; the threat of exile that causes more problems later; the romance Romeo is looking for; the excessive emotions that will cause problems throughout the play. It is an effective opening.

The first paragraph 'describes' only the important things that happen rather than everything that happened.

Look at the detail of the information given. Use names of characters/ places where possible.

Note the 'weighting' of this answer. The 'description' takes only one paragraph with the focus of the answer on the 'effect'.

Using the words from the question helps to keep you focused on the question.

It is important you not only state the opening is effective but tell why it is effective. Read the middle paragraphs of this answer and underline where this student suggests why the opening is effective.

An alternative way to answer this essay would be to choose three features of the opening scene you feel are effective and write a detailed paragraph on each.

DIY (DO IT YOURSELF!)

Now plan an essay that responds to the same topic using a text that you have studied. Aim to write a 250-350 word essay, making sure that you include reference to the text and suitable quotations. Make sure you choose a scene that is important enough for you to write about in detail. Always read the key words carefully and be sure that you understand what the focus of your essay should be.

ISBN 9780170244220

How to write a text essay on theme

Describe *an* ***important theme*** *in the text. Explain* ***how*** *at least* ***two production techniques*** *contributed to* ***your understanding*** *of the* ***theme****.*

Finding the key words

Any question that asks about the theme is asking about the ideas, message or purpose of the text. The above question is in two parts and you must address both parts to achieve well. You must respond to the chosen topic by commenting on it directly.

Structuring your essay

This essay question falls neatly into two halves. You need to be careful that your response addresses both parts of the question. After all, this section of your year's work is called 'show understanding' and it is the quality of your understanding of what you have read (or watched) that will determine your grade.

Make sure you have enough textual information to support your choice of theme and that you can draw clear links between it and the techniques you have chosen.

FINDING APPROPRIATE CONTENT

You will have discussed the theme/s of each text you have studied as a class and quite likely will have relevant notes or handouts in your folder. This would be a good place to start looking for information. In most cases you will have a choice as to which theme you use. Choose one that you feel most confident writing about or that you have the most information on.

You will need to begin by summarising your idea. This will involve stating the theme generally, explaining what it means and giving examples of how it can be applied to or seen in your text.

Make sure that you choose two techniques that you can see clearly impact on the theme of this text.

You can see that the two parts of this question require you to interweave the production techniques that the director uses with the theme that he or she is trying to communicate. A good essay will not separate the two elements of the essay. Below is a copy of the plan a Year 11 student created to help successfully structure their essay.

See how this student has thought about both the theme and the technique in each paragraph.

Paragraph 1. Introduction Theme – conflict: generations and East/West cultures
2 Techniques: costumes and music
Paragraphs 2. Costumes show generation conflict between Indian women.
Use Pinky's engagement party scene
Paragraph 3. Also show generations different attitudes. Use Jules + her mother
Paragraph 4. Introduce music/culture theme
Paragraph 5. Unhappy at home music, when grounded
Paragraph 6. Worlds come together, Indian music at soccer practice
Paragraph 7. Conclusion Conflict, costumes, music and me

ISBN 9780170244220

Crafting your answer

A little bit of careful thought and the essay is structured, it's easier to write and you'll get better grades. Here is the essay that grew out of the plan.

The film Bend It like Beckham directed by Gurinder Chadha has one major theme – conflict. It tells the story of an 18-year-old girl from an Indian migrant family living in modern day Britain. Jess (Jessminder Bhamra) lives between two worlds: the Eastern more traditional world of her parents and the Western world of the city that surrounds her. The conflict is connected to these two worlds but is also generational, between child and parent. This intergenerational conflict comes through in the English girl, Jules, life, too. The director has used both costume and music to help express these conflicts.

Title, director and main character's full name are given in the introduction. The theme is given in first sentence and chosen production techniques are listed. This tells the marker what to expect in the essay.

Jess's older sister Pinky, is getting engaged and the difference between the generations is illustrated in the clothes the women wear to the party. Both generations wear the sahler kameez, the traditional trousers and overdress, but the older women's ones are more modest, loose fitting, covering shoulders and upper arms, in patterned muted colours. The young women wear bold vibrant colours in off the shoulder designs to reveal their figures. Whilst this links them together as women from the same culture, it also divides them according to the extent they have assimilated into modern British life. These differences helped me to appreciate the theme if generation conflict because I can see the Western influences in the girls' clothing.

First example of a production technique (costume) is given in some detail. The paragraph ends with a sentence liking the description to topic, i.e. 'your understanding'.

I also saw it as a typical conflict between mothers and daughters, between generations in my own culture. This was further helped because similar conflict was shown between Jules and her mother. Jules wears her soccer uniform and unisex clothes all the time in the film, while her mother is desperate for her to dress in a more feminine way. When Jules goes to the wedding in a white top and track pants her mother is (wrongly) convinced her daughter is a lesbian. The mother's femininity is always underscored by her pink, patterned, frilly, silky costumes in the film. Costume points out their differences throughout the film.

Further examples of costume linked directly to writer's understanding, i.e. 'my own culture'.

Jess wants to play soccer; her mother wants her to learn to cook 'a proper Indian meal, meat and vegetarian'. The conflict between Jess's two worlds is also displayed through the way music is used in the film. Punjabi music plays in the Indian scenes, matching the events, so it

The second production techniques (music) is introduced. Several examples are given and again student remembers to include her own response as the question demands.

ISBN 9780170244220

sounds lively and happy at the engagement party, for example. Western music accompanies the 'English' scenes and the words reflect how Jess is feeling. For example, 'Independence Day' is the soundtrack when she escapes for a day to shop for soccer boots in London with Jules. Her mother thinks she is buying wedding shoes. Jess is starting to do things her own way – so the music supports this feeling. When I started to be aware of the music I could see how it helped me to fully appreciate Jess's feelings.

Further examples continue linked to climax of conflict.

When the English music plays behind her leaving her house in secret to play in a match, then it is adding to how her two worlds are colliding. The music also continues as her father attends the game so the music adds to the coming together of the two sides of Jess' life. Sad Indian music also backgrounds Jess cleaning her soccer boots and crying because she must go to her sister's wedding, not the soccer final. The music underscores her feelings again.

Shows student is in control of structure of essay.

Finally, with the conflict over, she is allowed to follow her dreams and the scene where she tells Joe this on the soccer field is backgrounded with Indian music. Her sport, her love and her family background are merging and the music reinforces this idea.

Simple direct conclusion.

Costumes and music are integral to the life and colour of this film, but they are also crucial in exploring the theme of conflict between cultures and between generations. They both extended my understanding of the way the conflict was so important in shaping the life of Jess Bhamra.

DIY (DO IT YOURSELF!)

Now plan an essay that responds to the same topic using a text that you have studied. Aim to write a 250-350 word essay, making sure that you include reference to the text and suitable quotations.

ISBN 9780170244220

How to write a text essay comparing short text

Although you are only required to use one text, you may wish to use more than one of the short text you have studied to answer a question. If, for example, you compare and contrast two shorter text you will have more material to use in your answer.

Here is an example of a question that you could use in this way.

> Describe at least one language technique in you text. Explain how the writer used language to show you an important idea in each text.

Let's take a look at how you could structure your essay.

STRUCTURING YOUR ESSAY

You will need to choose two text that have more than one feature you are able to compare and contrast. If you have features that both compare and contrast you should start by grouping them together. Divide your essay into two sections and deal with the features that compare first, and then the features that contrast. In a strong essay, you would be expected to write about at least three features.

You will need to start your essay by introducing the titles and authors of your two texts and perhaps indicating the similarities/differences you will talk about.

FINDING THE APPROPRIATE CONTENT

It is likely that you will have annotated copies of your texts in your folder from your close reading in class. You may also have handouts about your texts. You will need to start by sorting out the relevant information. Things to consider may include:

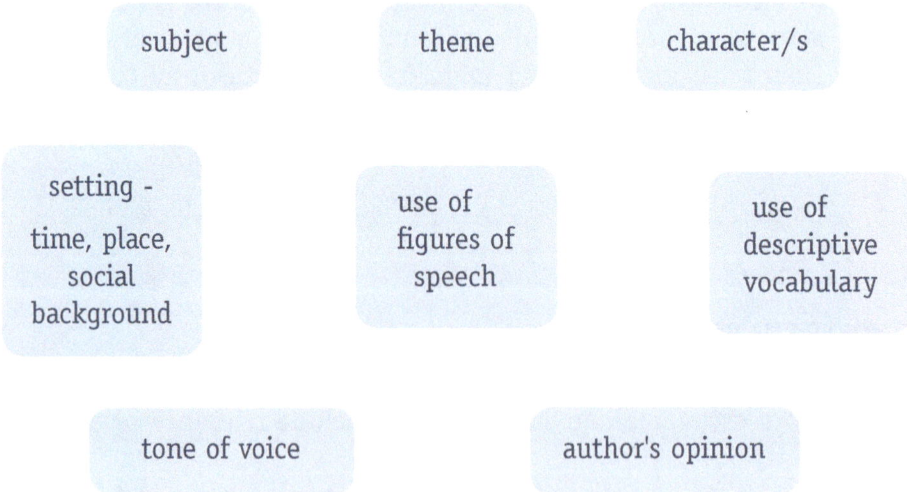

It can be very useful to know something about a writer's life when you are exploring his or her work. Use the Internet or a good biographical dictionary to search for such information.

ISBN 9780170244220

On the following two pages are war poems chosen by a student from a selection presented to the class. The poems show her annotations – the notes she made before planning and writing her essay.

Before beginning her task the student found this basic information about the two poets on the Internet.

Rupert Brooke (1887–1915)

Rupert Brooke was the son of a wealthy family, educated at Cambridge, and described as a good student and athlete and strikingly handsome. He joined the Navy, saw a little action but died of blood poisoning in 1915 en route to Gallipoli. His few poems are remembered as part of the 'inspired patriotism of the early months of war'. His poem *The Soldier* was published in 1915.

Wilfred Owen (1893–1918)

Wilfred Owen was the son of a railway worker. He failed to win a scholarship to the University of London and was working as a teacher of English in France when war broke out. He served in the army as a commissioned officer from October 1915 and was in the trenches at the battle of the Somme. He was killed in action seven days before the Armistice. Owen wrote several war poems now very well known, including *Dulce et Decorum est*, which was written in October 1917.

ISBN 9780170244220

published 1915, start of war

died 1915 early in war

The Soldier

first person narrator

how he wants to be remembered

If I should die, think only this of me:
That there's some corner of a foreign field
That is for ever England. There shall be
In that rich earth a richer dust concealed;
A dust whom England bore, shaped, made aware,
Gave, once, her flowers to love, her ways to roam,
A body of England's, breathing English air,
Washed by the rivers, blest by suns of home.

he is better than other nationalities … he is English

patriotic

pun 'sons'

And think, this heart, all evil shed away,
A pulse in the eternal mind, no less
Gives somewhere back the thoughts by England given;
Her sights and sounds; dreams happy as her day;
And laughter, learnt of friends; and gentleness,
In hearts at peace, under an English heaven.

Rupert Brooke

dies for a greater good

alliteration

abstract nouns …

soft vowel sounds

sonnet rhyme pattern: abab cdcd efgefg

deals with idealised future

ISBN 9780170244220

written Oct 1917 later in the war

Dulce et Decorum est

Wilfred Owen died 1918, fought in trenches.

Bent double, like old beggars under sacks,
Knock-kneed, coughing like hags, we cursed through sludge,
Till on the haunting flares we turned our backs
And towards our distant rest began to trudge.
Men marched asleep. Many had lost their boots
But limped on, blood-shod. All went lame; all blind;
Drunk with fatigue; deaf even to the hoots
Of disappointed shells that dropped behind.

similes – unpleasant comparisons

soldiers

We, I, my personal pronouns

personification

GAS! Gas! Quick, boys!— An ecstasy of fumbling,
Fitting the clumsy helmets just in time;
But someone still was yelling out and stumbling
And floundering like a man in fire or lime.—
Dim, through the misty panes and thick green light
As under a green sea, I saw him drowning.

personal experience narrating incident

simile

hard consonant sounds

In all my dreams, before my helpless sight,
He plunges at me, guttering, choking, drowning.

If in some smothering dreams you too could pace
Behind the wagon that we flung him in,
And watch the white eyes writhing in his face,
His hanging face, like a devil's sick of sin;
If you could hear, at every jolt, the blood
Come gargling from the froth-corrupted lungs,
Obscene as cancer, bitter as the cud
Of vile, incurable sores on innocent tongues,—
My friend, you would not tell with such high zest
To children ardent for some desperate glory,
The old Lie: Dulce et decorum est
Pro patria mori.

Wilfred Owen

simile

alliteration

concrete nouns

onomatopoeia

emotive alliteration

irony?

poet's opinions

patriotism

The phrase: *Dulce et decorum est pro patria mori* is in Latin. It comes from Horace's *Odes* written in the first century BC and means, 'It is sweet and becoming to die for one's country'. Owen calls it 'the old Lie'.

regular rhyme pattern, regular syllables too but not rhythmic

deals with reality of present

ISBN 9780170244220

Crafting your answer

Now look at how the student crafted an essay with the information selected.

The Soldier by Rupert Brooke and *Dulce et Decorum est* by Wilfred Owen

Both of these poems share a common subject: war and the patriotism associated with war.

Brooke, who died of blood poisoning en route to Gallipoli in 1915 and was not involved in much warfare, uses an English soldier narrator in his poem who is looking at the possibility that he might die in battle. He sees his death as symbolically leaving a part of England in the soil of the land where his body lies. 'In that rich earth a richer dust concealed'. He sees his remains as representing all the good that England is said to represent.

Owen experienced at first hand all the reality of war in the trenches. He too has a first person narrator 'As under green sea I saw him drowning' but this narrator is describing the young men all around him and how they look like 'old beggars' and 'hags'.

Brooke's poem concentrates on the positive, abstract things he sees England representing. Therefore England's strong young soldiers represent 'dreams, laughter, gentleness/In hearts at peace under an English heaven.' He is enthusiastic and sentimental about his homeland and all that the unnamed soldier is fighting to preserve.

Owen, who it must be remembered had seen much more of war than Brooke did, denies this sentiment, calls it 'the old Lie' and describes instead the horrific death from gas poisoning of one of his troop: 'the blood/Come gargling from the froth-corrupted lungs'. These are the things that will be remembered by those who fight:

> 'In all my dreams, before my helpless sight,
> He plunges at me, guttering, choking, drowning.'

Each poem uses its narrator to express the poet's opinion of war. Brooke's soldier wants the world to remember him as one who died in pursuit of an ideal:

> '... think only this of me
> That there's some corner of a foreign field
> That is for ever England.'

The manner of his death is never considered.

Owen's soldier, addressing those at home, tells those who encourage young men to join up 'children ardent for some desperate glory' of the 'vile incurable sores on innocent tongues' and instructs them not to repeat the old patriotic lies.

These two poets take the same subject, war and patriotism, but treats it in two completely different ways, perhaps because one experienced the reality of war and one did not.

Notice how the student has used the biographical information she downloaded from the Internet to add depth to the essay.

Poets choose their vocabulary very carefully. You, too, need to select quotations for your essay with great care. This student has chosen lines that directly contrast the two poets' styles.

There are conventions for quoting from poems. If you quote two complete lines they should be indented as shown. If a quotation is shorter but goes over a line end then that end is indicated with a forward slash: 'gentleness/ In hearts ...'

Notice the third section begins slightly differently by having a sentence introducing the feature being identified. Try using this technique yourself.

Notice that this essay is broken up into 'sections'. Each section looks at a different feature of comparison and includes two paragraphs, each dealing with one of the poems. An alternative structure would be to use only three paragraphs and deal with the poems/ poets together. You would need a clear lead-in sentence for each paragraph detailing the feature you are focusing on.

Note that this essay is about 370 words long. It has not considered everything, e.g. rhyme, metre, figures of speech. In terms of a Year 11 essay it is not possible to include everything. You need to be selective, as this student has been.

DIY (DO IT YOURSELF!)

Now plan an essay that responds to the same topic using text that you have studied. Aim to write a 250–350 word essay, making sure that you include specific detail and quotations from each of your chosen text.

ISBN 9780170244220

7

Formal Writing

We know you have heard it all before, and it is a toss-up whether to say it all over again, but as teachers we couldn't bring ourselves not to! So, as quickly as possible, here is a re-cap of the structure of a formal essay:

1 Introduction

You will need an introduction that:

- states your argument or topic
- introduces your main points
- tries to grab your audience's attention.

2 Body

You will need to have at least three paragraphs in the body of your essay that:

- cover logical arguments
- are in a logical order
- start with your strongest point and end in your weakest
- do not say the same thing in three different ways.

3 Conclusion

You will need to have a conclusion that:

- restates the main points of the essay
- reinforces the writer's attitude without introducing any new information
- gives a strong, though-provoking statement or question as a final sentence.

It is that simple, really!

However, there is a little more to it than that. Read on!

Planning

Before you begin any piece of writing it is always essential to plan – a formal essay is no different.

You will be rewarded when the marker can see where the writing is going right from the start. They call this 'controlling' the essay. It is important that you spend as much time working out the points you are going to make and what pieces of evidence you will need to back them up, as you do writing and crafting the piece.

ISBN 9780170244220

Breaking it down

We assume you have done some formal writing in the junior school. It may have been a letter to a principal or member of your local council, it may have been a review on a text you studied in class or as part of your personal reading.

When producing a piece of formal writing at Year 11 you are frequently asked to present your opinions about a certain topic. (You may be asked to write an article for a publication, or write a letter expressing your viewpoint for a publication, but it all means the same thing.) At this stage we are going to 'teach' you how to write a formal piece of writing that argues a point or persuades your audience to agree with your point of view.

No one is a born writer – it is a skill that is practised and refined. However, it is possible to improve your skills with a few 'tricks of the trade'. We are going to break the structure of an essay down to small chunks so that you can learn how to write the different parts of the essay and how best to utilise your information. At that stage you can build an essay of your own.

The introduction

Why do you need an introduction?

Your introduction will 'introduce' the reader to your essay. It will indicate all the things you are going to write about and suggest the angle you are going to take. From your point of view it will help you structure your essay and keep it on track. Sometimes writers will use attention-grabbing techniques in their introduction such as:

- an emotive statement
- a controversial statement
- a rhetorical question
- a surprising statistic.

A simple introduction has three parts

The function of each part of an introduction is as follows:

1 It echoes the question/topic.
2 It states the point of view.
3 It introduces the main points.

TASK 1: ANNOTATING AN INTRODUCTION

Below is an introduction for an essay on the topic 'Zoos should be abolished'. It follows the guidelines above. Circle the sentences that cover each part and write the number for each next to it.

> There are only about 800 giant pandas in the world and the 80% who live in the wild in China are constantly threatened by poaching and habitat changes. If it weren't for zoos protecting 120 pandas they could soon be extinct. Therefore zoos should most definitely not be abolished. They offer an educational experience to their visitors. They help to recover the numbers of many endangered species and zoos offer homes for animals whose natural habitats are being destroyed by humans.

ISBN 9780170244220

TASK 2: ORDERING AN INTRODUCTION

Below are the sentences of an introduction for the essay 'Family is more important than friends'. Unfortunately they are not in a logical order. In the space provided write a logically sequenced introduction using all of these sentences.

Everyone has family: brothers, sisters, mum, dad, grandma and grandpa, step-dad or half-sister perhaps.

When things get tough family is more important, more long-lasting than friends.

My friends are there for the good times, to go to the rugby with, to hang out with at lunchtime in school, to chat to on the telephone.

Do I have to? Every teen has asked the question, usually after being told he or she has to go on a family outing.

But when there's a problem, when I feel sick, when my cat dies – then I need my Mum.

The body

The most important part of your essay is what is generally referred to as the body. This is where the bulk of your ideas and opinions is expressed/presented.

What the body of your essay needs to do:

- Discuss each point made in the introduction in turn.
- Keep your argument going.
- Keep on track by referring back to the initial topic.
- Give supporting detail to back up what you say.
- Be organised in a local manner.
- Be paragraphed carefully.

Obviously you will need to structure the 'internal workings' of the essay as well as the essay as a whole.

We are sure you have been told that 'a new idea gets a new paragraph'. Most likely you will come up with three or four points about a topic. Each of these points will need to be taken separately and clearly explained in a paragraph of its own.

A paragraph can be seen as a miniature essay. Think of it as arguing just that point rather than the whole topic. You need to state the idea, support the idea and conclude the idea within that paragraph before you move on to the next one. Once you have learnt the basic structure of paragraphing writing you will find essay writing much easier. In fact those of you who are confident writers will be able to play with the structure for effect.

ISBN 9780170244220

Why is it important to paragraph?

- It shows you are organised.
- It makes your argument easier for the reader to read and understand.
- It signals a new point is being made.
- It reminds us to separate one point from another.

Each paragraph can be prepared in the same way as you prepare the whole essay. You may use systems like GEE or SEX in your classroom. Here is an alternative process that you can try.

1 Lead Sentence

What are you writing about?

- This sentence 'introduces' the paragraph.
- It states the main ideas of the paragraph.
- It may link to the previous paragraph.
- It will link to the topic of the essay.

2 Explanation

What do you mean?

The next sentence/s will explain what you meant by your lead sentence.

It is where you give your reader more detail, lots more detail about the idea you are expressing.

It will use key words from your paragraph idea/or from the topic of the essay.

3 Evidence

What makes you say that?

The next sentence/s will give the evidence, the proof, the examples to support the idea you have explained. It may offer:

- Statistics
- Survey results
- Anecdotes
- Examples from the media
- Personal experience.

You will, of course, use different types of evidence in different paragraphs.

4 Relevance

So why is all that important?

The final sentence/s of the paragraph will convince the reader that your idea in this paragraph supports your approach to the topic of the essay.

It will probably link back to the first sentence of the paragraph.

It will certainly link back to the topic of the essay.

ISBN 9780170244220

Have a look at how a paragraph written by a student has followed the structure of the grid for the topic **'New Zealand benefits from its many cultures'**.

1 Lead Sentence

What are you writing about?

New Zealand benefits from this cultural mix in many ways, but especially in the way our economy is stimulated and helped to grow by our ability to do business with the outside world.

2 Explanation

What do you mean?

We have people who work in business who speak the language and understand the culture of other countries. For example, if a company is doing business with China then having employees who speak Chinese and understand Chinese culture must be beneficial.

3 Evidence

What makes you say that?

Problems that might occur through inaccurate translations, for example, can be avoided.

4 Relevance

So why is all that important?

Our cultural mix strengthens New Zealand's trade with the outside world.

ISBN 9780170244220

Taking a step back – deconstructing a paragraph

Here is the next paragraph from the essay on **'New Zealand benefits from its many cultures'**. However, the sentences are not in a logical order. In the grid below write the sentences in the sequence the student should use.

We can enjoy festivities of other cultures, sharing food, music, traditions that other cultures have developed over centuries, things that we would have to travel halfway around the world to enjoy if we were not a multicultural society.

We would have to go to China to experience this if we did not have Chinese people living here.

This is a benefit to our social life, giving us much more choice in entertainment.

For example, the Chinese community in Auckland shares its lion dances, dragon dances, opera, food and lanterns every year during the Chinese New Year.

New Zealand also benefits at a social level by having a multicultural society.

Lead Sentence	**What are you writing about?**
Explanation	**What do you mean?**
Evidence	**What makes you say that?**
Relevance	**So why is all that important?**

ISBN 9780170244220

Putting it all together

This essay needs a third paragraph. We have given you the lead sentence. You do the rest.

Lead Sentence	**What are you writing about?** *Another good reason why New Zealand benefits from its many cultures is the way this can help us overcome racial intolerance.*
Explanation	**What do you mean?**
Evidence	**What makes you say that?**
Relevance	**So why is all that important?**

ISBN 9780170244220

An aside on ... tone

One of the things that the marker will be watching for is whether you use a tone that is appropriate to both the style of writing and publication for which you are writing. You will have been given the chance to write creatively if you were assessed for 1.4. Produce creative writing. Now is the time to prove you can adopt a formal tone and write appropriately.

You need to imagine you are writing to someone deemed to be in an important position – your principal, a member of local government, and so on. You would not write to them in the same way you would talk to your mates in the school grounds. This means removing any colloquial conversational terms out of your writing.

However, as always there is an exception to the rule. Those of you confident with writing may choose to use informal language for effect. Unless you know you can 'carry it off' we suggest you leave this until you've had a bit more practice.

An aside on ... vocabulary and linkages

We want you to consider your vocabulary (word choice). We are not expecting you to swallow a thesaurus but you might like to try incorporating some of these words and phrases into your next essay.

BEGIN PARAGRAPHS:

- Furthermore
- Moreover
- In addition to
- Also

TO EMPHASISE:

- Obviously
- In fact
- As a matter of fact
- Indeed
- In any case
- In any event
- That is
- Surely
- This example clearly shows ...

TO BEGIN YOUR CONCLUSION:

- In brief
- On the whole
- To conclude
- In conclusion
- Finally
- The fact is that ...
- In the light of ...

INTRODUCE YOUR EVIDENCE:

- For instance
- One such example is ...
- To demonstrate
- To illustrate
- As an illustration
- Evidence for this can be seen
- A recent example was
- In recent years ...
- In many cases
- It has been said
- It has been reported ...
- At the present time ...
- ... has been quoted saying ...
- Recently

TO SUMMARISE OR USE TO BEGIN YOUR CONNECTING SENTENCE:

- Accordingly
- Hence
- Therefore
- Consequently
- As a result
- Since
- Because
- Then
- Owing to
- Thus
- It seems
- It is therefore clear
- As a result of this
- Nevertheless

TO REPEAT:

- In brief
- In short
- As I have said
- As I have noted
- In other words
- However
- Arguing that
- It is claimed that
- According to this position

OTHER USEFUL PHRASES:

- Unfortunately
- Younger generations
- The question is
- Of course we all know about ... but
- Currently
- It seems that
- The public are familiar with ... but
- There is a general perception that
- In today's society
- This example proves

Avoid using 'firstly, secondly, thirdly'. Maybe use this device once one in an essay, but if you use it at the beginning of each paragraph it sounds repetitive and unsophisticated.

ISBN 9780170244220

The conclusion

Why do you need a conclusion?

It is just as important to have a carefully planned conclusion as a carefully planned introduction. It is the last thing that the marker will read and you want to leave a strong final impression. A conclusion ties the points together.

A common trap students fall into is to finish an essay too quickly. The end is in sight and so they dash off two lines that just repeat the introduction. It is very important to do more than this. Your conclusion should sum up your essay, but not rewrite it. The conclusion should logically follow on from the points you have made and should never bring in any new information. Your conclusion should be convincing your reader that your ideas and point of view are the best ones. It's also a good idea if the lead sentences are reworded in a slightly different way so that they don't sound as if they are being repeated.

A simple conclusion has four parts

The function of a conclusion is as follows:

1 It echoes the question
2 It gives a strong, thought-provoking statement/question as a final sentence.
3 It reinforces the writer's point of view
4 It re-states the main points without introducing any new information.

TASK 1: ANNOTATING A CONCLUSION

Below is a conclusion for an essay on the topic 'Zoos should be abolished'. It follows the guidelines above. Circle the phrases/sentences that cover each part and write the number for each next to it.

In conclusion there is a definite place in this world for zoos and similar establishments. They provide a platform for people to interact with and see animals that, without zoos, they may never be given a chance to see. Zoos are heavily involved in breeding programmes, which will ensure the survival of many endangered species and they help animals to live in a safe habitat where their food and environment is not being destroyed by humans. So save animals – don't abolish zoos.

TASK 2: ORDERING A CONCLUSION

Below are the parts of a conclusion for the essay 'There are too many gambling options available in New Zealand', which are not in logical order. On the lines below, write a logically sequenced conclusion using all of these parts.

- *We are teaching our children to provide for their own enjoyment and not for the family's wellbeing*
- *In conclusion, the strain of casinos, TAB Sports Betting and Lotto is having a detrimental effect on New Zealand.*
- *This lunacy needs to stop.*

ISBN 9780170244220

- *Violent crimes are increasing.*
- *Unless the New Zealand government puts an end to gambling, our future as a nation faces a rocky path.*
- *So are financial difficulties.*

An aside on ... topic choice

Now that you've seen how an essay can be put together we need to deal with the biggest difficulty of all: What do you actually say? How many times have we heard students say 'But what do I say?' or 'I know what I'm trying to say but I can't get it down on paper'? All the structure in the world doesn't help you actually come up with the ideas!

Many students find writing an essay difficult because they choose the wrong topic to start with. Half the knack of having something to write about is in the choosing of the topic. Here are a few things to think about:

- Do you pick the first topic that interests you?
- Do you pick the first topic because you can't be bothered to read on?
- Do you pick the visual topic because it catches your eye first?
- Do you pick the 'cool' topic because you get 'fired up' about it and end up waffling?

If you answer 'Yes' to any or all of these have a look at the next list.

- Do you carefully read all the topics through first?
- Do you mark those that you know something about?
- Do you then go back and think about the general knowledge you have about any of the topics?
- Do you eliminate any bad choices?
- Do you write a few quick notes about a couple of topics to get a 'feel' for what you know?
- Do you pick the topic that you are best prepared to answer?

It is always important to think carefully about the topic you choose. The lists above might have helped you recognise a few of the traps students fall into.

Let's take a look at how you might come up with your points keeping in mind that at this stage we are leaning how to write an essay so you will be given more time to come up with ideas than in an examination.

ISBN 9780170244220

Stop and take a look ...

Below is an essay written by a Year 11 student under examination conditions. It achieved an Excellence.

TO GET AN EXCELLENCE THE STUDENT NEEDED TO HAVE:

- Several sensible ideas. Highlight the main idea from each paragraph.
- Relevant examples to support his ideas. Using a different colour to highlight the examples.
- Key words from the topic in his essay. Using a red pen circle the words taken from the topic.
- More than the minimum number of words. Count the words.
- A formal style. This is a formal essay written in a formal style. Do you recognise a formal style?
- An accurately written essay. This student can spell! It helps!
- A persuasive style that commands attention. Can you see that this essay is easy to read and has ideas that show common sense?

Rugby is too dominant in New Zealand

Rugby is a national sport in New Zealand and is even considered as the identity of New Zealand. But when is it taken too far? New Zealanders have become fanatically obsessed with rugby over the years. New Zealand has neither enough money nor enough interest to sustain other sports and New Zealand boys may actually feel pressured into playing and enjoying rugby.

Rugby has been New Zealand's national sport throughout history and a passion for it has always been there. However, nowadays, this passion has evolved into a fanatical obsession with the sport and everything to do with it. Rugby players are now featured in the majority of television advertisements on New Zealand television. Frequently talked about, they are now idolised. In Shakespearean times the rank of king was the highest status: in New Zealand today, being an All Black is its equivalent. The obsession has advanced so much that now there is a phone line developed to match people's faces to an All Black's face. New Zealanders have to get their priorities into perspective. Rugby will always to be our national sport, but it cannot take over our lives.

This obsession with rugby can be seen in how there are insufficient funds and interest in other sports. The fact that the majority of sporting people in New Zealand play rugby and netball could see the extinction of many other sports, due to the lack of interest. Unfortunately, even with willing participants, New Zealand may not have enough money to sustain other sporting codes. This has already started occurring, as there are concerns that there may not be enough money to send the Black Sticks, the New Zealand men's hockey team, to compete in the Olympics. It is not fair that money is being spent excessively on

ISBN 9780170244220

rugby, and now other sports people are suffering. New Zealand needs to open its mind to all the other sports, and not stunt the opportunities of other athletes.

Today, in New Zealand, it is almost expected that very young boys play rugby. Many boys are pressured, either by family, friends or society in general, to play rugby. If he does not enjoy it he has to pretend to do so, to avoid being ridiculed. This is not a healthy atmosphere, nor an ideal way to grow up. Sports are meant to be enjoyable, something each individual chooses for himself or herself. If a young boy was pressured into playing rugby, he would have missed out on the benefits that truly enjoying a sport gives you. He may even grow up resenting sports, which isn't a good image to pass down to children.

Rugby is indeed much too dominant in New Zealand. People have become much too obsessed, putting rugby ahead of other more important issues. The money and interest put into rugby could lead to the extinction of other minority sports. And finally, a young boy can be easily pressured to conform to society and be forced to play rugby. New Zealand needs to open its mind and broaden its horizons. Rugby may be the national game but it does not have to be the only one we play.

An aside on ... looking for evidence

It is vital in an essay, whether it be a literary essay on a specific character, a geography essay on urban sprawl or an expository essay arguing a point, that the writer provides proof for his or her argument.

Many students find this difficult but there are many places you can go to find your examples:

- Use the internet
- Use newspapers
- Use an encyclopedia (old fashioned we know but there are many specialist encyclopaedia that may help you)
- Use organisations
- Use the vertical file
- Use magazines
- Use people (your parents!)

Think about who you would approach about the topic if you were doing a research assignment. For instance if you were arguing the benefits of having all public places as smoke-free who might you talk to? A smoker? A non-smoker? The Cancer Society? ASH? FADE? A restaurant owner?

It is also important to remember that there is a wealth of examples available from your own life. Often you will be given a topic about a teenage issue, for instance cellphones, part-time work, fashion, body piercing. You will either know about how others have reacted to the issue or have had first-hand experience yourself. It is not important that you admit you are talking about your own life; word it as being someone else if you want.

Whatever you do, it is not enough to state a point and skim over it – examples that support your point are essential.

ISBN 9780170244220

Creating an essay

You guessed it. It is time to write your own essay. We thought we'd help you out a bit though. You will see that parts of the essay have been written for you. Your task is to complete the essay in the grid provided.

Topic: Physical Education should be compulsory from Years 9–13.

Introduction	*Physical Education is an important part of the school curriculum and should be made compulsory for Years 9 to 13.*

Lead Sentence	**What are you writing about?** *Physical Education encourages students to continue being active and healthy throughout their school life.*
Explanation	**What do you mean?**
Evidence	**What makes you say that?**
Relevance	**So why is all that important?**

ISBN 9780170244220

Lead Sentence	What are you writing about?
Explanation	What do you mean? *By playing sports and fun games students learn to trust each other and work together in a team because they can't win by themselves. They build respect for themselves and other people and learn to get on with people who otherwise they may never have spoken to.*
Evidence	What makes you say that?
Relevance	So why is all that important?

Lead Sentence	What are you writing about?
Explanation	What do you mean?
Evidence	What makes you say that? *For instance my brother was interested in sailing at Year 13 at school and he is now 23, a member of a sailing club which keeps him fit and gives him a strong friendship group with people with a common interest. If he hadn't tried sailing at school I don't believe he would have found this sport by himself.*
Relevance	So why is all that important?

Conclusion	*Physical Education is a valuable part of schooling and students should be made to make the most of this subject.*

ISBN 9780170244220

Finally ...

Before you write a complete essay on your own have a look at what the markers want. No doubt you have heard it all before.
The Assessment Report for Formal Writing makes comments that will not surprise you. Markers are looking for evidence of planning; good ideas, which can be supported well; a formal style of writing and accurate spelling and punctuation.

None of this is new to you. However, take a look at some of their more detailed comments:

IDEAS

- *... ability to develop a sensible, strong argument supported by relevant, commonsensical detail, at times displaying real insight into an issue ...*

Translation

- Choose a topic you know something about. Plan before you write. Use examples from real life: yours and the life reported in current affairs (not movieworld!) Think about what is happening in the world around you in preparation for this essay. Use things you learn about in other subjects, perhaps.

STYLE

- *... ability to write in formal style. A colloquial or conversational style, at times using direct address, is inappropriate for this standard ...*

Translation

- Do not use slang or colloquial language. Write in the third person ('It is necessary...' rather than 'You should...'). This is your writing in its best clothes: clean, pressed, everything matching.

STRUCTURE

- *... ability to structure their writing: divide ideas into paragraphs with a clear introduction and conclusion ...*
- *... ability to use an effective structure, often with an interesting original introduction that linked well to a striking conclusion ...*
- *... ability to indicate a progression of ideas with linking phrases ...*

Translation

- Having an introduction, three points in three paragraphs and a conclusion is great. For Merit or Excellence it's the way these are linked together that counts.

CONVENTIONS

- *... ability to use sound sentence structures, spelling, and punctuation ...*
- *... ability to write with reasonable technical accuracy ...*
- *... ability to proof-read and edit their writing ...*

Translation

- Accuracy in spelling, punctuation and sentence structure matters – it always matters.

An aside on ... proofreading

Whenever you write an essay it is important to build time into your work for proofreading. Every writer, professional or amateur, needs to read over his or her work. For students at your level it is particularly important that you check all your sentences. Accurate spelling, punctuation and paragraphing make your writing easier to read and understand.

ISBN 9780170244220

Practice writing assessment: 'Education is fuel for the future'

Your task is to compose a 400-500 word formal essay based on this topic. Remember to think and plan first. If a grid like the one on pages 125-127 will help, make one for yourself.

Note: Do not fall into the trap of copying these all out in the hope that that will do. Use them to help you form ideas, possibly incorporating some of these as your examples.

It's your Future calling ...

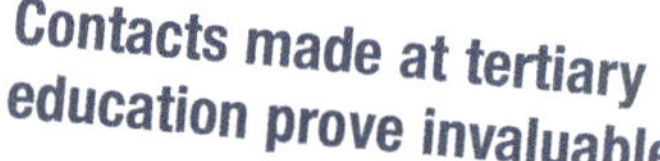

'Education is not only academic, it can be physical, mental, personal ...'

'leading the way to a rich future'

starts here

'NZ has the highest level of participation in degree level education in the OECD'

Ministry of Education

Personal Growth

Get ready, go

Top of the class; top of the pay ladder

NZ students get top marks in reading and maths

NZ school students are among the top international class for literacy and numeracy, according to a report made ...

Go further with education

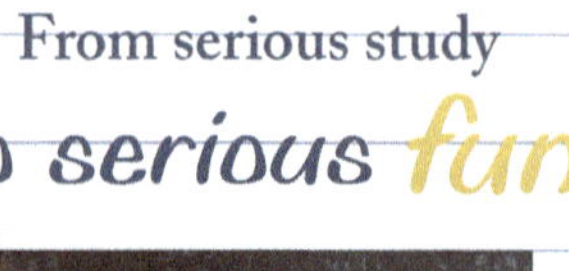

Shaping your future

ISBN 9780170244220

Making your Visual Text

This year you will quite likely be asked to produce a Visual Text. You will be expected to construct an image that uses appropriate language and visual techniques.

There are key things that you need to keep in mind when designing your own image:

1 Audience

As with any text you read, analyse and create, the intended audience is an important element. You must always take the audience into account so that you use techniques that are likely to attract that particular group. They may be female or male, teenagers or older people, ethnic groups or drunk drivers, sports shoe buyers or movie-goers.

This year it is likely that your official audience will be your peers. However it is important that you still meet the requirements of your assessment, as your second audience will be the person who marks your work.

2 Language techniques

Most images have a written component to them. It may be one word, one line, a short paragraph of body copy or a combination of them all. Any words that appear on an image need to be carefully chosen so they help you get your message across.

If your static image is based on a text you have studied in class, you may be asked to include a relevant quotation. You will need to return to your notes on the text and perhaps even the text itself to find exactly the right words that fit your static image.

Think about using: alliteration, cliché, emotive language, grammar, hyperbole, imperative, neologisms, personal pronouns, pun, repetition, rhetorical questions, slogan, tone, statistics etc.

3 Layout techniques

How the words and pictures of an image have been put together is an important element of static image design. Professional designers position nothing on the page accidentally but rather everything is placed in order to create a unity of ideas and to let the viewer's eye move naturally from the most important feature to the least. You will need to carefully plan the layout of your image to be successful.

Think about using: balance, dominant visual feature, empty space, rule of thirds, hierarchy, perspective, proportion, border etc.

4 Visual techniques

In order to grab the audience's attention you will need to look carefully at the visual techniques you use. This may be done by using provoking pictures, bright colour or bold lettering. In most cases, we will be attracted to the 'look' of an image and hopefully we will then be drawn enough to study it in detail.

Think about using: bold lines, colour, contrast, lettering, pictures/illustrations, reverse print, symbol, unusual images, well-known/popular faces etc.

5 Message

The basic aim of an image will be to influence us to act a certain way or make a particular decision. In Year 11 it is likely that your image will be required to reveal your personal understanding of a text you have studied in class. It may also influence the way other people who have read the same text respond to it. Although you are not producing an advertisement, you will be using the same techniques to that media designers use to get their message across.

Remember, you need to make sure you are doing more than simply drawing a picture!

6 Overall impact

Your image needs to stand out from a crowd of other images. Designers are always trying to make their image the most noticeable and memorable. One great way of getting some ideas is to look with fresh eyes at the walls of the classrooms you spend time in every day. Remember imitation is the sincerest form of flattery. If you see a great presentation technique used on another student's poster, you may well be able to adapt it for your own work.

ISBN 9780170244220

Before we go any further ...

Visual text – test yourself

Fill in the gaps using the terminology in the box below.

well-known people	rhetorical question	cartoon	cliché	pun
superimposing	personal pronouns	symbol	message	font
target audience	empty space	impact	border	colours
dominant visual feature	reverse print	body copy	contrast	layout

1. A ______________ is a play on words to give a double meaning.
2. When words are printed in white on a black background it is called ______________ ______________.
3. When designing a static image, it is important to always keep the ______________ ______________ in mind.
4. A ______________ is used to represent something.
5. When an image (or part of one) is placed on top of another it is called ______________.
6. Different ______________ can be used to represent feelings or actions.
7. Areas of ______________ help to make features stand out.
8. One way of making the audience feel that the image is directed at them is by using ______________ ______________.
9. The element of an image that stands out the most is referred to as the ______________ ______________ ______________.
10. The term used to describe how different elements of a static image are arranged is ______________.
11. A ______________ helps to keep the viewer focused on the image by giving it an edge.
12. An over-used, hackneyed expression used in everyday speech is called a ______________.
13. A pencil outline drawing is called a ______________. It is often used for humour or satirical effect.
14. It is important to choose a ______________ that is appropriate for the writing on your image.
15. For an image to be successful it must have ______________.
16. A ______________ ______________ invites the reader to think about the issues in the poster.
17. It is not necessary to completely cover your static image. ______________ ______________ can also be effective.
18. Some images use the faces of ______________ ______________ to endorse a product.
19. Several sentences of small type are referred to as ______________ ______________.
20. The most important function of a static image is to get the ______________ across.

ISBN 9780170244220

Critical thinking

At Year 11, your visual text must demonstrate that you have done some critical thinking. Let's demonstrate for you how one Year 11 student has done this. The class was required to produce a visual text based on *Tomorrow, When The War Began* by John Marsden. Just in case you don't know this great story, it is concerned with a group of Australian young people who are isolated from their homes and family by war. The main character is a teenage girl who has to learn to be courageous. She discovers that courage requires thinking, planning, strength and sometimes extreme actions that would be unthinkable in peacetime.

When you have looked at the image, read the student's words to see if they add more meaning for you.

ISBN 9780170244220

My visual text is on 'Tomorrow. When the War Began', by John Marsden. I have chosen to represent the theme of courage. Ellie Linton is one of the main characters. She starts off as a young girl on holiday going on a camping adventure with some mates. She is young, free and looking forward to nothing more than a few days away with her friends. By the end of the novel she is an independent, seasoned warrior who is fighting for her freedom, her family's freedom and the freedom of her country.

I wanted to get across the idea of what Ellie had to do to stay in control and not let all the things that were going on around her driver her to give in.

I chose the quote 'I was a mess of different feelings. I wanted to be able to make calm, logical decisions ... but I couldn't get my feelings out of the road enough to do it' because it illustrated how confused and stressed Ellie was throughout the book.

The quote is written in red because I wanted it to stand out from the rest of the image.

The background of my image is a montage of barbed wire, flames and wire fencing. These things represent elements of the war that are going on around her. It is coloured in reds and oranges to help suggest the chaos happening around her and her loved ones.

My dominant visual feature is a black silhouette of Ellie. It takes up 2/3rds of the image in order to make it dominant. The colour black also contrasts with the orange/red background.

I wanted to show what Ellie had to learn in order to be courageous. I used a series of nine symbols to do this. The symbols were in a grid because to be able to act bravely Ellie had to compartmentalize all the conflicting emotions and demands on her, to be able to think before she acted and remain in control of herself.

The symbols are:

Group of people: This represents the friends that Ellie had in Hell. She needed to stay calm because these people saw her as a leader and she needed to keep their morale up.

Fear: The word 'FEAR' has been written in shaky lettering to suggest how scared Ellie actually is. It represents the fear that Ellie had that she had to keep to herself or she would panic and not be able to think straight.

Book with the 'Survival Guide': this represents the fact that Ellie had to think in order to survive. They needed to think about the things they needed to stay in Hell and therefore stay alive.

Australian flag: Ellie was fighting for her country.

Heart: Ellie couldn't let her heart rule her actions.

House: This represents Ellie's home. She hated to see what the invaders had done to her farm and she desperately wanted life to go back to how it had been before the invasion.

Exclamation mark: This represents the danger Ellie was in.

Her family: Ellie knew her parents were imprisoned in the fair ground and she needed to both remember that she was fighting for their freedom but forget them as she didn't need any distractions while she was fighting to remain alive.

Blood pool/gun: This represents all the things that Ellie did that she didn't want to have to dwell on as they were horrible for someone her age to have experienced. Ellie had to shoot one of the enemy (hence the gun) for her friends to survive. If Ellie thought about this too much she would not be able to go on.

I think that I have produced a cohesive image that clearly explains how Ellie managed to be such a courageous fighter and role model for those around her.

We think this student's explanation will have enhanced your understanding of the image. We also think if you write a similar explanation of your own image it will ensure that you have communicated as clearly as you can.

Hopefully you will have learnt several things by looking at this student's work. The first is that she has drawn more than a picture in order to represent courage. She could have easily drawn the scene where Ellie shoots the enemy. Or she could have drawn the scene where the tanker is blown up. But both these things would only have been just that - a picture.

To create a successful image you must go beyond the obvious and look deeper at what is happening to either the characters or the story.

This can be a frustrating and time-consuming part of creating your image but when you have a clear idea you will find it easier to move on. Plan to use lots of paper, screw up lots of bad ideas and go back to the drawing board again and again. Use the experience of your teacher to help you. Obviously they will not be able to tell you what to do but they can give you guidance as to whether you are on the right track and tell you when you have reached the point of success!

ISBN 9780170244220

Time to make your own ...

There are things that we want you to think about before you start producing your image

- Planning is the key.
- Go back to your notes and read them through.
- Think about your 'response' to these themes.
- Choose one that you feel you understand well.
- Select an appropriate quotation that illustrates your theme.
- Remember, perhaps not the entire quote is necessary. Write only the relevant parts and use an ellipsis (...) to show where you have left words out.

Aside: we suggest that you plan two images ... one will usually end up stronger than the other but having thought of two will often help you think better.

There are things you need to think about when you have your final theme/quote

- How are you going to lay this out?
  Will your page be landscape or portrait? Will your writing be at the top or the bottom? Think about the rule of thirds, creating balance etc.
- How are you going to use the space effectively?
  Empty space can be effective but only if it is planned that way. Think about the proportion of your elements. If it is an A3 image, it is no good having illustrations that are the size of a credit card.
- How are you going to source the images?
  Photocopy something and then trace or draw? Magazines? Avoid using the 'head' from a magazine photograph and drawing a body ... it looks unprofessional.
- What colours are you going to use?
  Will they contrast? Be used to represent emotion/s?
- What font will you use?
  Style? Capitals? Lettering book, from the computer and then trace to colour paper and cut out? Montage using magazine cutouts?

There are things you need to think about during the production

- Make sure you have all the gear you need
- Make sure you are accurate
- Make sure you are tidy
- Make sure you are careful
- Make sure you are sticking to plan
- Make sure you are using your time wisely.

There are things you need to think about at the end of your production

- You will need to outline your lettering etc in a fine black ink pen so that the letters stand out and are defined.

IMPACT

IMPACT

- A simple ink (or twink if black background) border helps to keep the eye on the page and give your image a finished appearance.

ISBN 9780170244220

Your design

Use this page to work on your final design. Use the grid on the following page to keep track of the techniques you use and the reasons why you are planning to use them.

ISBN 9780170244220

The title of my text is ______________________________

TECHNIQUE	WHERE USED	WHY USED

ISBN 9780170244220

9 Presenting a Speech

Ladies and Gentlemen, my speech this morning is about speechmaking. Um ... oh no I remember I'm not supposed to say that. That's a filler. I'm supposed to know better than that. I'll just read this from my cue paper. Don't worry if I'm not looking at you, it just means that I'm terrified. Hang on a minute. I'll say just straighten up my spine because I've just remembered that I'm supposed to stand straight and tall. Forgive me for fidgeting, I know I'm not supposed to do that. Oh, I just used alliteration. That's a technique. I might get a mark for that. Can you hear me at the back? I'm pitching my voice to you.

Sorry if this seems a little boring. I would have had a PowerPoint display but the dog ate my speech and I was running late and my USB drive didn't work on the teacher's computer.

You'll see how I just flung my arm out to one side there. I'm trying to use a gesture to try and direct you to look at the teacher's computer.

I'd like to pause here ... because it will use up another 30 seconds of my speech.

Pause ... What do you think of my speech so far? That's a rhetorical question. Did you notice?

I seem to have covered everything I have ever learnt about making speeches. Which is:

Bullet, bullet, bullet (listing) ...

So let's see if I can improve on this.

(STANDS STRAIGHT, SHOULDERS STRAIGHT, DROPS PIECE OF PAPER, PULLS CUE CARDS OUT OF POCKET AND HOLDS AT WAIST LEVEL THEN LOOKS AT THE AUDIENCE.)

Ladies and Gentlemen, my speech this morning is about speechmaking. Many Year 11 students hear the word 'speech' and freeze (she holds her body position for three seconds). Actually it is a great opportunity to have your say while everyone HAS to listen to you. After all, we all have an opinion that we'd like others to share, don't we?

It is important to actually have something to talk about, that's true. Those of us that can't get beyond what my cat did yesterday are going to struggle! But even that little topic can be expanded. Think about all the programmes on TV that talk about training belligerent pets to behave. Now there's a speech topic. You'll need to do some research – but hey, that's what the Internet is for. And after all, we've all been writing formal essays forever and the structure of a speech isn't all that different, is it?

Really, that's the easy bit. If you have to give your speech on a Friday you should really have finished writing your speech on the Monday to give yourself several days to practise to your baby sister, the mirror, the family dog (they don't criticise!), and if you're really desperate, Mum and Dad!

There is no doubt it helps to practise where your ex-ag-ger-ation (not to mention pause, voice intonation, gesture, eye contact blah, blah, blah) (tick off on fingers) is going to be used.

In the words of Nike ... just do it ...

YOU KNOW WHAT WE MEAN, DON'T YOU?

You've probably seen and heard a lot of not-so-great speeches. Let's look at some ways of making your speech the best it can be.

ISBN 9780170244220

Before we go any further ...

Speeches – test yourself

Unfortunately this list of dos and don'ts has been mixed up. Place a tick (✓) or a cross (✗) to represent whether you think each one is a good idea or a bad idea.

1. Don't use pauses. It is better to use filler words like um, er and ah. ☐
2. Know your audience and ensure your speech has some relevance to them. ☐
3. Read your speech word for word from a piece of paper. ☐
4. Talk quickly to ensure your audience does not fall asleep. ☐
5. Use statistics but don't overdo it. ☐
6. Rehearse your speech out loud in front of a mirror. ☐
7. Use distracting industry jargon. ☐
8. Limit your topic. Pick a simple idea and develop it. ☐
9. Fidget or play with something like a pen or pencil while you deliver your speech. ☐
10. Use visual aids whenever you can to hold your audience's attention. ☐
11. Talk past your time limit, losing the audience's attention. ☐
12. Use your hands self-consciously. ☐
13. Keep eye contact with people in the audience. ☐
14. Outline key points on cue cards so you can stay on track. ☐
15. Write an opening statement that will intrigue your listeners. ☐
16. Speak clearly and loudly enough so that your voice can be heard by everyone. ☐
17. Use humour to help win over the audience and make your speech stand out. ☐
18. Panic if you make a mistake. ☐

ISBN 9780170244220

Techniques in speeches

Whether it be a persuasive, informative or entertaining speech, all speeches will use the same techniques to get their message across. Remind yourself of these techniques in the diagram below.

SPEECHWRITING TECHNIQUES USED TO …

… APPEAL TO THE AUDIENCE

- personal pronoun
- rhetorical question
- emotive words
- informal language
- use of humour

… BACK UP AN ARGUMENT

- anecdotes
- listing
- quotations
- references to authority
- use of humour

… MAKE YOUR SPEECH MORE INTERESTING

- alliteration
- metaphor
- simile
- rhythm
- repetition
- imperatives

… MAKE YOUR SPEECH SOUND LOGICAL

- structure
  - beginning
  - middle
  - end
- bridging words and phrases
- links between introduction and conclusion

SPEECH PRESENTATION TECHNIQUES USED TO …

… KEEP AN AUDIENCE INVOLVED

- voice intonation (pitch/speed/inflection)
- eye contact
- posture
- knowing your speech
- facial expressions
- props
- SMILE!

… EMPHASISE A POINT

- gesture
- tone of voice
- pause

ISBN 9780170244220

An aside on ... 'choose whatever topic you want'

If you are faced with a complete vacuum, the 'write your speech on whatever you want' instruction, then let's see if we can give you a helping hand.

Category one:

- Speak about something you know about: break a big topic into something that is more focused.
  - Rather than thinking 'I've got younger brothers and sisters, I'll write about them' think about 'How do I cope with having three ankle biters living in my house'.
  - Rather than 'the environment' think about 'Where do all the dead computers go?'
  - Rather than 'Sport is good for you' think about 'Basketball is just as important as rugby'.

Category two:

- Use everyday life as a source of inspiration.
  - A day in the life of a Wattie's Spaghetti can ...
  - Getting to school unscathed.

Category three:

- Getting serious. Rather than thinking in sweeping generalisations look for current issues in the news like:
  - Waste management
  - Developing new energy sources
  - Reducing crime
  - Pollution in New Zealand waters

It really is our best advice that you make a speech about something you are interested in. You will sound more passionate, more involved, more expressive if you actually care about what you are talking about.

Understanding speeches

Before you write your own speech it is a good idea to stop and look at how other students have tackled the task.

Student speech 1

READ THIS SPEECH written by a Year 11 student (granted he was quite good at this!).

AS YOU READ IT THROUGH THE SECOND TIME, ANNOTATE:

- Links between beginning and ending
- Structure of the formal essay i.e. beginning, middle, end
- Bridging words and phrases

As teenagers we hold one thing above all others. One thing we cannot live without. One thing we spend most of our hard-earned cash on.

This object is highly regarded as our way to communicate, our way to keep in touch with parents, friends, employers ... everyone really. What is this one indispensable thing? Need I tell you? It is this *[produce phone]* – the cellphone. My cellphone; my small, stylish, splendid, spectacularly useful cellphone.

ISBN 9780170244220

But there's a dark side to this amazing little communication device. And it's not the cellphone's fault. 'Text bullying' is a phrase that has entered the language and the lives of lots of young people. For every person who uses the cellphone in a positive way to keep in touch with friends and family, there's another who uses it to cause misery to others.

Gone are the days when students avoided certain areas of the mall, certain toilet blocks in the school, avoided certain routes home. Physical bullying, which might have occurred in such places, has a new mate – text bullying. Though they're probably performed by much the same sort of person. Text bullies just have far more opportunities to create misery and they can bully from a distance, anonymously. They don't need to hang about in the loo any more. Text bullying can happen anywhere, anytime, and once it starts it is not easy to make it stop.

Text bullying happens when someone is mean to another person by text. It's not something that just happens, it is words created by a real person and that person is as unpleasant a human being as the big physical bully who punches someone smaller than him or herself. A text bully's messages might be rude, scary, mean, or just something weird that makes the recipient feel a bit gross or uncomfortable.

People who bully others are often cowards, the word 'bully' is defined as 'coward and tyrant' in the dictionary, and being a text bully is especially cowardly because the text bully feels anonymous and safe, as their victim is out of sight. Texts can be sent after school, at night, and even on weekends so the victim feels as if there is no place or time to be safe.

Text bullying is no different from physical and mental bullying: it involves targeting one person and saying abusive and offensive comments to the victim to make them feel bad about themselves. It is not unusual for a group of people to get together and bully one person in particular. This is referred to as 'ganging up on' someone. The word 'gang' fits these bullies. Victims of text bullying may be bombarded with messages, often using extreme language, 24/7. That's any time, any place, day or night.

This is not a small problem. It is not a once-in-a-while event. Last year, Vodafone alone received 4600 complaints about text bullying. That's over four thousand people feeling bullied to the point of making a complaint!

But that is just the tip of the iceberg. Sometimes the text bullying goes further than making a young person scared or feel pressured into doing something, and becomes more serious. A young girl had to be removed from her school because of all the merciless text bullying she was receiving. She would break down in tears during class time, and she threatened to commit suicide on several occasions, telling her family and her teachers that she could not face her own life any longer. The worst case scenario of text bullying is when someone is pushed so far, that they do actually commit suicide. There are even documented cases here in New Zealand.

ISBN 9780170244220

Is there anything being done about this? Surely people aren't being left to deal with this alone?

It is true that there are many things that the victims of text bullying can do to help themselves. If you receive an unpleasant text message from a text bully, don't text the bully back. It's very important not to get sucked in to their world. You might feel like sending the person who is bullying you a text to make them feel as bad as you do. By doing this, you'll become a text bully! It's a much better idea to ignore the message. Don't reply, but save the message on your phone, so that you can go on to step 2.

Step 2 is to tell an adult that you trust. If you are worried about having your phone taken away from you if you tell, most adults know that being text bullied is not your fault. Sometimes just sharing this problem with a trusted adult is enough to help you handle the problem.

You can contact your service provider, that's probably Vodafone or Telecom, if this is happening to you. "We're very concerned about reports of TXT bullying and are committed to helping young people fight this," says Vodafone general manager of communications and sponsorship Lynley Kirk-Smith.

If you receive four or more messages in a week, and you don't reply to them, Vodafone or Telecom can disconnect the bully's phone from the network permanently and in some cases the victim can get a new number.

Organisations like NetSafe want to make sure that young people don't feel helpless and ensure that they're aware of the practical steps they can take to help themselves if they are dealing with text bullying. NetSafe runs a hotline for people who are being text bullied. This helpline can provide counselling and sensible advice such as: watch out who you give your number to. Also, do not reply to any messages from senders you do not know, because bullies can send out random texts and see who replies. How weird is that?

One of the worst things we all can do is to allow bullies to keep being mean. If people are too scared to tell on them, whether they be victims or peers of the bully, these unpleasant people keep getting away with it. It's really important to tell someone so that the bully won't get away with it. All bullying is serious, but nasty texts that can be sent fast and anonymously by anyone to pretty much anyone whose phone number they have, is especially serious.

So, text bullying – I am prepared to bet that there is more than one of you right here today who has had an unwelcome text message. As teenagers we need to make sure that collectively we say, "It's not OK". We have to support the victims of text bullying by listening to them, assuring them that the bully is a coward, that ignoring mean words is the right thing to do, and that telling a trusted adult is the best way to keep safe. We must dob in the perpetrators, make sure people know where to go for help and how to stop this scourge. Let's try and delete text bullying from our language and our lives.

ISBN 9780170244220

AS YOU READ IT THROUGH THE THIRD TIME, HIGHLIGHT TECHNIQUES SUCH AS:

- Personal pronouns
- Rhetorical questions
- Colloquial language
- Alliteration
- Anecdote
- Statistics
- Use of quotation
- Listing
- Emotive language
- Repetition
- Cliché

READ IT A FOURTH TIME

But read it aloud, thinking about HOW the speech would be delivered. Mark on the speech (using the symbols in the box below) places where you would use voice or gesture to deliver the speech in the most interesting way.

Annotation marks for speech delivery

Mark	Meaning
______________	Underline words to be emphasised. Make the line darker if the words need to be emphasised very strongly.
/	Mark where you need to pause with a slash. You can also use this to identify where to breathe in a particularly long sentence.
←——→	When you need to speak more slowly (perhaps to emphasise a phrase) use an extended arrow to remind you to extend the time it takes to say the words.
------------------	Use a dotted line below anything that needs to be said quickly.
↑	Use an up arrow if you need to raise your voice in order to emphasise or draw attention to a certain phrase.
↓	Use a down arrow if you need to lower your voice. Also use this mark if you tend to raise the intonation of your voice at the end of sentences – doing this at the end of every sentence is a Kiwi habit that turns every sentence into a question – try to avoid it!
g or *	Mark where you can use a gesture with a g or *. Eventually gestures will become a natural part of your performance but until then you may need a memory jog. You can write the gesture in the margin if you wish.
E or an eye shape	Mark where you must make eye contact with an E or an eye shape. It is very important to look at your audience.

YOU DO:

Choose a 30 second segment of this speech. Practise it to present to the class. You are to present the segment well, and then repeat the same segment showing how a bad speech would be presented.

(Note: This is an excellent way of seeing what makes a good speech. Try it!)

ISBN 9780170244220

Student speech 2

Here is another speech written by a Year 11 student. The topic is more humorous so the student uses speech techniques in a different way in order to achieve his purpose. Read the following speech carefully and answer the questions that follow.

Is Santa Real?

He's the jolly fat guy with the red suit, flying over your house in a red sleigh pulled by eight reindeer. Good morning ladies and gentlemen, my speech is on, that's right ... Santa Claus, Old Saint Nick, Kris Kringle.

For many years now, confused children between the ages of 8–12 years have been asking themselves whether or not Santa Claus is real. Today I hope to help answer that question.

The facts are stacked heavily against the poor old guy. For a start there are 2.18 billion children in the world. Out of that roughly 15 per cent are from cultures or religions that don't celebrate Christmas. This leaves 1.85 billion children who expect to receive presents from Santa Claus. Now this means that he and his elves have to make 5,065,068 presents a day. An astronomical number I think you'll agree.

Secondly, he has to fit all these presents into one ridiculously small sack, then fly around the world towed by eight floating reindeer. He will need to make approximately 1.23 billion stops at various houses around the world. And finally, the earth has a circumference of 32,000 km, but Santa does not fly in a straight line. On no, he flies from here to there, travelling 62,000 km. Of course this is a ballpark figure, as his sleigh's speedometer is broken. He has to travel this staggering distance in 24 hours, meaning he will be going no less than 43 km per second. That's all very well but the problem is if he were to travel at that speed he would burn up in the earth's atmosphere. At each stop he has to climb down very small chimneys. An almost impossible challenge for his oversized gut and himself.

On the other hand, Santa may have millions of elves working for him and each one is extremely productive. He may also have found some way of freezing, or at least slowing down time. And why not coat himself in Vaseline to stop him burning up? As for Rudolph and his seven companions, Santa may have found some way of breaking free of the chains of gravity. After all David Copperfield did. Who says he has to go down chimneys? Maybe he is a master criminal and capable of picking any lock, dropping off the presents and sneaking out, quiet as a mouse whilst we are fast asleep.

I took the liberty of asking a few people whether or not they believed in Santa Claus. Upon approaching my parents and forwarding the question to them, I was politely told to 'get real'. I won't even bother repeating some of the other replies.

Just remember to spare a thought for that hard-working, fast-flying, overly busy fellow who, whilst you are out celebrating Christmas Eve, is fast at work keeping children of the world happy. So I'll let you decide whether Santa is really an over-generous, misunderstood old man, or a mass advertising campaign.

Bryce Caird

ISBN 9780170244220

1 Identify the following in the Santa speech by annotation (underline and note the term in the margins).

rhetorical question	involving the audience
colloquial language	use of humour
quotation	simile
use of statistics	listing

2 Annotate the speech where you best see the student using the following:

Gesture for added interest	Gesture for emphasis
Facial expression to match words	Eye-contact to establish rapport
Intonation for reinforcement	An area to speak – slowly – quickly – loudly

3 Choose a 30 second segment of this speech. Practise it to present to the class. You are to present the segment well, and then repeat the same segment showing how a bad speech would be presented.

(We repeat: this is an excellent way of seeing what makes a good speech. Try it!)

An aside on ... a few tips on using PowerPoint

Some of you may choose to use PowerPoint to help you illustrate your speech. Don't plan to use it as an excuse to not to know your speech or have cue cards but rather use it for effect. For instance it may be useful to have an emotive photo behind you, a map or diagram that helps explain what you are saying. Take a look at the following guidelines to help you create your slides.

- Choose the background colour of your slides carefully. A dark background and light font work the best.
- If you have text on your slide choose a font that's easy to read. Arial, Tahoma or Trebuchet are usually recommended.
- Use bullet points so that you use as few words as possible.
- Look at your audience, not at your PowerPoint, when you speak. Eye contact is still important.
- Stand on the right side of the projector – we tend to look at the screen from left to right and if you are standing where the eye begins you are a bit of a distraction yourself.
- Use as few slides as possible: less is more
- Give your audience a moment to digest what is on each slide when you open it
- Use gesture to direct audience attention to what you want them to notice
- But keep you body half turned to the audience even when gesturing or pointing to a slide
- Say things that link the slides together, e.g. "Now, let's look at..."
- Stand away from the light from the projector!
- Make sure the equipment is working before the audience arrives.

In *How to ... Achieve in Year 10 English* we took a closer look at how to use Powerpoint effectively. Go back and refresh your memory if you need to.

Remember ... PowerPoint doesn't communicate – you do!

ISBN 9780170244220

Your speech

Use this page to work on your final speech. Use the grid on the following page to keep track of the techniques you use and the reasons why you are planning to use them.

TOPIC: ______________________

TECHNIQUE	WHERE USED	WHY USED

ISBN 9780170244220

Language Lists

Although we have divided these techniques into lists linking them to specific text, they may well be relevant to more than one type of text. For example, you might find a rhetorical question in a speech, a formal essay, a poem or a magazine article.

Language techniques for written text

NOUN
Naming word.
E.g. plum, Peter, power, pod

COMMON NOUN
Name of ordinary, everyday objects. Can be preceded by 'a/an' or 'the'.
E.g. a pear, an apple, the banana

PROPER NOUN
Name of person, place etc. Always begins with a capital letter.
E.g. Alan to Zebedee, Africa to Zanzibar

ABSTRACT NOUN
Name of something that we cannot see, touch or measure. You can give it ...but you can't wrap it up.
E.g. air, authority, amazement

COLLECTIVE NOUN
Name of a group of objects, people or creatures. A *collection* of similar things or people – that is why it's called a *collective* noun.
E.g. band, orchestra, ensemble, quartet, group

PRONOUN
A pronoun is used in the place of a noun. Avoids always repeating a name.
E.g. I, me, mine, you, yours

ADJECTIVE
An adjective describes a noun. Adds detail to names and nouns.
E.g. black, bold, big, brave, bronzed

COMPARATIVE ADJECTIVE
A form of adjective that compares things. Shows the difference between two things.
E.g. blacker, bolder, bigger, braver, more bronzed

SUPERLATIVE ADJECTIVE
A form of adjective that describes the best or the most from three or more things. It's also pointing out difference.
E.g. blackest, boldest, biggest, bravest, most bronzed

VERB
A word that expresses doing or being. Somebody or something does something. Something or somebody is something.
E.g. I eat, I drink, I am (happy), I was (thirsty)

ADVERB
Gives you more information about a verb. Adverbs tell you when, where or how something is done.
E.g. cheerfully, thirstily, happily, miserably

CONJUNCTION
A conjunction links two or more sentences into a single sentence. Known as a 'joining word'. Conjunctions are usually found in the middle of sentences, but not always. Conjunctions can also join words, phrases or clauses.
E.g. and, so, but, yet, or, after, because

PREPOSITION
A preposition tells us the position or place of something in relation to something else. Prepositions are usually 'small words'.
E.g. at, by, for, on, in, of, under

EUPHEMISM
A euphemism expresses an unpleasant or uncomfortable or embarrassing situation in a more sensitive, kind and tactful manner. The purpose is to soften the blow, protect feelings or to be politically correct.
E.g. My grandfather passed away.

PUN
A pun is a clever play on words which are similar in sound but different meaning. The double meaning is used to convey humour. Puns are often used in headlines, advertising, jokes and riddles.
E.g. P&O holidays: living the cruisy lifestyle.

CLICHÉ
Trite and worn out phrases that communicate an image easily, and don't need too much thinking about.
E.g. I could eat a horse.

COLLOQUIAL LANGUAGE
The word colloquial is used to define language that is used in casual conversation. It is likely to be even more ungrammatical, fractured and full of cliché than informal language. You will use colloquial expressions in your everyday conversations with friends and family.
E.g. G'day. You coming out? I'm off now.

ISBN 9780170244220

SLANG
Slang is very informal language that is usually vivid, playful and short-lived. Each generation formulates its own slang and these words are usually 'passing phases'. We would have given you an example but it would be out-of-date before the book was printed!

JARGON
Jargon is used by a particular group, profession or culture. Often, other people do not understand the words and so it can seem like pretentious or meaningless language. Jargon may be highly technical.
E.g. My new bike is awesome. It has a Cro-mo frame and alloy rims and the groupset are all high spec'd. I got semi-slicks but they threw in some knobblies, too.

See also: Language Techniques for Poetic Text

Language techniques for poetic text

IMAGERY
The creation of images or pictures to help writers achieve their intended purpose. An image can be created using different devices such as similes, assonance or adjectives.

SIMILE
A simile is a direct comparison that always contains the word 'as' or 'like'.
E.g. My brother John eats like a pig.
This suggests that John has unpleasant table manners. A simile adds vivid, descriptive details.

METAPHOR
A metaphor is a comparison which does not use like or as. It says that one thing is another.
E.g. My brother John is a pig
This metaphor suggests that John has unpleasant manners, not that he actually is a pig. Metaphors are used to highlight certain qualities of whatever is being described.

EXTENDED METAPHOR
This is a metaphor that is extended over a passage or throughout a poem.

PERSONIFICATION
Personification is where a non-living object is given living qualities, writing of it as if it were a living person. Appearances, actions, thoughts and feelings can all be given human attributes. Personification gives life and energy to images and ideas.
E.g. The vine is strangling that tree.
This gives the idea of the vine as an aggressor with intent to harm and the tree as the victim.

ALLITERATION
Alliteration is the repetition on consonant sounds at the beginning of words placed closely together to create a sound echo.
E.g. A black-backed gull bent like an iron bar slowly
This line has to be read slowly in order to pronounce the words. Therefore it emphasises the strength of the wind against which the bird is flying.

Alliteration is used to:
- add humour or power
- create a mood or feeling
- help the flow or movement of language. Some alliteration is hard ... b and d, while others are soft, calming ... l, s, f
- emphasise important points

ONOMATOPOEIA
Onomatopoeia uses words that imitate and reproduce real-life sounds and actions.
E.g. The buzz of a chainsaw.
Onomatopoeia helps to increase reality in the text through adding another dimension by suggesting sound as well as meaning. Onomatopoeic words are often found in comic strips.

ASSONANCE
Assonance is the repetition of vowel sounds. The trick is not to think of it as the same letter, but the same sound.
E.g.
He climbed high, singing wildly
Clinging to the rock face
Alive, at last.
As with alliteration, assonance allows the poem to flow more quickly or it can slow the poem down as each word is emphasised to reflect the meaning of that part of the poem. Note: assonance is not rhyme! In fact true assonance is where the consonants following the vowels are different.

RHYME
Rhyme is the repetition of final vowel and consonant sounds in words.
E.g.
She left the web, she left the loom,
She made three paces thro' the room,
She saw the water-lily bloom,
(from The Lady of Shallot, Alfred Lord Tennyson)
In this poem the rhyming words at the end of each line match well the rhythm and harshness of the poem's meaning. Words that sound the same, or almost the same, are likely to make us notice them. Rhyming words can fall anywhere, in the middle of lines, in regular or irregular patterns, but we are most used to them at the end of lines of poetry.
Rhyme is designed to:
- add pleasing sound effects
- provide a disciplined structure
- highlight particular words/phrases
- follow an established pattern.

RHYTHM
The rhythm is the flow and beat of the poem.
E.g.
This is the night mail crossing the border
Bringing the cheque and the postal order
(from The Night Mail, W.H Auden)
Here the beat/sound of the train is imitated.

ISBN 9780170244220

REPETITION

When words or phrases are repeated for emphasis of some kind.

E.g. Veni, vidi, vici. I came, I saw, I conquered.
(Julius Caesar)

Repetition is often used for emphasis and in this case Caesar is pointing out his own importance.

Language techniques for visual text

CONTRAST

Use of two colours for eye-catching contrasts. Designers think about which colours combine effectively. For instance yellow & black, red & black, orange & purple.

E.g. Football team uniforms.

DVF

The Dominant Visual Feature is the central focus of the static image. The point of impact. It may be dominant because of its position, often at the centre of the image.

GRAPHIC/ILLUSTRATION

Graphics are the pictures, photographs, drawings, graphs – everything that is not the writing in an image.

WELL-KNOWN/POPULAR FACES

Many advertisements use someone who is famous to sell a product/service. It may be purely to attract attention *(for example Daniel Carter selling underwear)* or it may be endorsing a product that the celebrity would know about *(for example Tiger Woods advertising golf clubs)*.

FONT (STYLE AND SIZE)

Designers choose the fonts of the text to go with their images carefully. The text must be clear to read (not too elaborate) and in some situations, able to be read from a distance. The font will also aim to reflect the ideas within the image.

E.g. In advertising a children's product the font will be large and colourful while a funeral home is likely to choose an elegant, simple font.

COLOUR

Colours help represent a product or an idea.

E.g. An advertisement for berry yoghurt is likely to be based around pinks and purples to help represent the product. An image designed to sell a cleaning product is likely to have a lot of white to suggest cleanliness.

BOLD LINES

Bold shapes and lines help to draw in the eye. Some things are outlined in black to give them definition or to frame certain parts of the whole image.

BACKGROUND

The background may be left plain in order to focus the viewer's attention onto the other features or it may incorporate colour to support its message.

E.g. A green background on an advertisement for a healthy product is not uncommon, for example, as green suggests natural. Faint images which link to the message of the whole poster or advertisement may be used as background.

UNUSUAL IMAGES

Unusual pictures or layout to make people stop and study the image more closely may be used.

SYMBOLS/LOGOS

Symbolism is where a concrete object is used to represent one or more abstract ideas. It can be words, a shape, a graphic.

E.g. The dove (a material object) represents peace (something abstract). White crosses may represent road accident victims.

Most companies and services have a logo (graphic drawing/symbol) that represents their company, from the Nike whoosh to the MacDonald's M.

In the same way that 'a picture is worth a thousand words' so a symbol or a logo can bring to mind a whole range of thoughts and feelings.

LAYOUT

Layout is the process of organising forms, shapes, colours and any words into a balanced design. These choices are made with the purpose, topic and audience in mind.

THE VERBAL/VISUAL LINK

Whenever a visual text is put together there is always a strong focus on the links that exist between the verbal and the visual elements.

BALANCE

Designers achieve balance by looking at a layout design as an arrangement of shapes. The easiest way to create balance in a visual text is to treat all the elements as geometric shapes.

RULE OF THIRDS

The rule states that an image can be divided into nine equal parts by two equally-spaced horizontal lines and two equally spaced vertical lines. The four points formed by the intersections of these lines can be used to align features in a visual image.

Designers believe the Rule of Thirds creates more tension, energy and interest in the image than simply centering the feature would. Following the rule also helps produce balanced picture/images.

EMPTY SPACE

Empty space refers to areas of the text that have no text or graphics in them. These areas may not necessarily be printed in the colour 'white', but it is important the colour is the same throughout so that the effect works in the same way.

Empty space is used to:

- prevent the layout looking crowded
- help balance the overall design
- create impact or focus on a certain feature
- help the audience to read the text and graphics in the correct order.

HIERARCHY

The hierarchy of a layout design means the order of importance of different elements and the order in which elements should be viewed or read. When each element is given a grade of importance and designers style or

ISBN 9780170244220

size them as such, it makes it easy for readers to know where to look or read first and where to move their eyes across and into the visual.

HEADLINE

The headline is the main 'title' of the advertisement/image. This will be in the biggest font size. Subheadings, in smaller print, may be used, too. The words are designed to attract attention and provoke the audience to look further.

LEVEL OF LANGUAGE (FORMAL, INFORMAL, COLLOQUIAL, SLANG, JARGON)

The type of language chosen for an advertisement gives us clues about the intended audience.

- If it is simple it could be aimed at children.
- If it is feminine and flowery it is most likely aimed at girls or women.
- If it is chatty and conversational it is most likely advertising something we would use everyday.
- If it is formal it is most likely advertising something of a serious nature.
- If there is a lot of technical language it would have a very specific audience in mind, for example modern computer users or car fanatics.
- A lot of slang terms might indicate it is aimed at a youthful audience.

REPETITION

Repetition aids memory, whether it is to donate money to World Vision or to buy Five Brothers pasta sauce. Repeating the product name, slogan and/or key features will help people remember the brand.

PUN

A pun is a clever play on words, using two words that are alike in sound but different in meaning. The double meaning is used to convey humour. Headlines make use of puns in order to grab attention.

E.g. Trust British Paints ... Sure Can.
New Indian Restaurant Curries Favour

USE OF ADJECTIVES

Advertisers will often choose words that help us picture the look, taste or texture of the product. Think about what advertisers say about breakfast cereals: *crunchy, wholesome, nutty, tasty*.

Comparative adjectives like *'better'* and *'kinder'* and *'creamier'* are often used.

Superlatives are common, too. Think about the words *'crumbliest, flakiest'* which are superlative adjectives. You are probably thinking Cadbury's chocolate!

SLOGAN

Most companies and services have a slogan (a short, snappy sentence) that is easy to remember. You probably know where it is claimed that 'everyone gets a bargain'.

BODY COPY

Body copy is usually found in a paragraph towards the bottom of an image. These detailed words in a static image are often referred to as the 'small print'.

RHETORICAL QUESTION

A rhetorical question expects no answer because it assumes one. It is used to allow the audience to focus on and consider the posed question.

E.g. Sick of spending hours scrubbing your shower and it still not being clean?

The assumed answer to this question is 'Of course, I am.'

PERSONAL PRONOUNS

Personal pronouns are used to make the audience feel that the advertisement is speaking directly to them. They give a chatty, conversational tone to the piece to make the audience feel included.

ALLITERATION

Alliteration is easy to remember. The audience will be able to recall the catch phrase at another time. Alliteration also makes words flow together more easily and it can highlight key words and ideas.

E.g.
Just Juice
NZ Natural

Language techniques for speeches

RHETORICAL QUESTION

A rhetorical question is a question where the answer is implied. It adds to the persuasive power of the speaker. Often a speaker adds emphasis to a point by putting it in the form of a question, the answer to which supports his or her argument.

Rhetorical questions are designed to get the audience to momentarily stop and think about what is being said. This in turn involves them in the speech and encourages them to keep listening so they can hear what the answer will be. It is essential for there to be a pause after a rhetorical question to allow this thought to take place.

E.g. What is this one indispensable thing? Need I tell you? It is this – the cellphone.

A rhetorical question may also be used effectively at the beginning or end of a speech. It either engages the audience immediately or leaves them with something to think about. This may provoke them to make a change in their lives or to consider the issue beyond the end of a speech.

PERSONAL PRONOUNS

A speaker uses personal pronouns to involve his or her audience. By using 'you' the speech comes across as being aimed directly at the audience, as though the speaker is talking to individual members of the audience.

'We' and 'our' are also commonly used by a speech-writer to encourage the audience to think the speaker is one of them and therefore makes them feel included. This in turn makes the speech seem more personal.

E.g: 'As teenagers we hold one thing above all others. On thing we cannot live without. One thing we spend most of our hard-earned cash on.

ISBN 9780170244220

LISTING

Listing is where speakers will 'list' several examples at once. Providing an audience with a lot of examples adds weight to your argument. It is also an economical way of getting a lot of information across quickly.

E.g. 'My cellphone; my small, stylish, splendid, spectacularly useful cellphone.'

QUOTATIONS

Quoting well-known people may give a speech a greater air of authority.

Quotations work well at the beginning or end of a speech as they can make people pay more attention to the idea being expressed.

E.g. '"We're very concerned about reports of TXT bullying and are committed to helping young people fight this," says Vodafone general manager of communications and sponsorship, Lynley Kirk-Smith:'

EMOTIVE WORDS

These are words which have strong feelings, or emotions, associated with them. These emotions can be positive or negative. Such words set the **tone of voice** which expresses the speaker's attitude to a person or topic. E.g. 'sunny, hopeful and healthy' versus 'grim, disgusting, and dangerous".

Positive words create a sense of confidence and optimism about an argument. Negative words can suggest disapproval or pessimism.

E.g. 'A young girl had to be removed from her school because of all the ***merciless*** *text bullying she was receiving.'*

USE OF STATISTICS

Using statistics helps to support ideas with fact. They can convince the audience that there is verifiable support for an argument.

E.g. 'Last year, Vodafone alone received 4600 complaints about text bullying.'

ANECDOTES

Telling a short story (based on either fact or fiction) can help to illustrate a point. Speakers often use these to keep their audience interested and listening because we all enjoy stories.

E.g. 'A young girl had to be removed from her school because of all the ***merciless*** *text bullying she was receiving She would break down in tears during class time, and she threatened to commit suicide on several occasions ...'*

REFERENCES TO AUTHORITY

Referring to people, groups or companies that have authority helps make the audience believe your claims as they know the source is reputable. Groups such as the Police, United Nations, Governments, Greenpeace, Amnesty International fall into this category.

E.g. 'Organisations like NetSafe want to make sure that young people don't feel helpless and ensure that they're aware of the practical steps they can take to help themselves ...'

INFORMAL LANGUAGE

Chatty, colloquial phrases help relax the audience and make them feel involved. Speech-writers will often use clichés, contractions, colloquial phrases in order to do this.

E.g. 'How weird is that?' ...

REPETITION

Speech writers (just like poets and visual designers) employ the repetition of words or phrases in order to emphasise a main point. It may be a point repeated several times throughout the speech to ensure that it is emphasised or it may be the first word or phrase repeated for emphasis.

E.g. Gone are the days when students ***avoided certain*** *areas of the mall,* ***certain*** *toilet blocks in the school,* ***avoided certain*** *routes home.*

USE OF HUMOUR

One of the most powerful tools a speech-writer has is humour. We all like to laugh. It must be appropriate to the subject matter though.

E.g. 'My cellphone; my small, stylish, splendid, spectacularly useful cellphone.'

See also: Language techniques of poetic text

Techniques for film

Types of shots

A **shot** is taken from when the camera is **turned on to when it is turned off.** Shots are defined chiefly by the distance of the object from the camera. Here are some of the more common types of shots you will be asked to identify:

ESTABLISHING SHOT, EXTREME LONG SHOT (ELS)

Contains a lot of landscape and gives important information about the setting, atmosphere or context in which events following the shot will take place. An establishing shot is often used at the beginning of a scene or sequence and gives an overall picture, placing the characters in their settings.

LONG SHOT (LS)

Contains a significant amount of landscape or background though figures in the scene are recognisable as being human and male or female.

FULL SHOT (FS)

Contains the whole height of any figure in the frame.

MEDIUM SHOT, MID SHOT – (MS)

Where the person is seen from the waist up. Medium shots allow you to observe facial expressions and body language such as tension. They also show reactions between characters.

If there are two people in the shot it is called a two-shot, if there are three people, a three-shot.

CLOSE-UP (CU)

Contains no background but focuses on the whole of an object or a person's head and shoulders. Close-ups are used to show whatever is most significant at any given moment and focus our attention on it. They may reveal human emotions or private information.

ISBN 9780170244220

EXTREME CLOSE-UP (ECU)
Focuses on an aspect of an object in fine detail or a part of a person's face, headline of a newspaper or detail of symbols, such as a police identification.

OVER-THE-SHOULDER SHOT
Where a shot is filmed over a character's shoulder, from behind. It is usual for this shot to look towards another character and will generally be followed by a reverse-angle shot showing the face of the person whose back was to the camera. It is mostly used during conversations or interviews.

POINT OF VIEW SHOT (POV)
Where the camera becomes the eyes of one of the characters and sees things from that character's point of view. The director may want viewers to identify with this point of view.

Camera angles

HIGH ANGLE SHOT
Taken when the camera is above or looking down at the figure. The main purpose of this shot is to make the object or person look small, insignificant or helpless.

LOW ANGLE SHOT
Taken when the camera is below or looking up at a figure. The main purpose of this shot is to make the object or person look large, powerful and dominant.

OVERHEAD SHOT
Taken when the camera is directly above the figure. This suggests insignificance or isolation or vunerability.

UNDER SHOT
Taken when the camera is directly underneath the figure. This suggests extreme power or danger.

Camera movement

PAN
A camera 'pans' when it moves horizontally (side to side) on its tripod. It is often used to show the vastness of a location.

TILT
Where the camera moves upwards or downwards on its tripod to follow moving objects or reveal a scene or object which is too big to fit in one frame.

TRACKING
The camera (mounted on tracks, vehicle, dolly or hand-held) follows the subject. You will frequently see this shot used during a 'chase' scene as it makes the camera appear to be following or 'tracking' the object: it makes the audience feel like they are alongside the action.

ISBN 9780170244220

Use this space to list any additional language techniques introduced to you by your teacher.

ISBN 9780170244220

11

It's time to Revise – get over it!

It is the time of the year that you need begin considering how you are going to approach the external assessments for Level 1 English.

We know ... you know ... everyone knows that no matter what kind of student you are, NOW is the time to begin REVISION.

There are several things you need to decide:

WHERE ARE YOU GOING TO WORK?

It is important that you set yourself up a study station. You will need a desk or a table, a comfortable (not too comfortable) chair, good lighting ... and quiet. Make sure you have a good stock of refill, pens, pencils and highlighters, too.

If you are not able to work in your bedroom, then using a corner of the dining room table is fine. Turn off the TV. Turn off the radio. Ask Dad to take care of your little brother. You need time and space to think!

WHEN ARE YOU GOING TO WORK?

You probably have lots of things in your life other than school. This is the time of year when you evaluate which of these things are unavoidable and which commitments could be put on hold (or at least reduced) during the lead up to the examinations. Can you work fewer hours? Do you need to attend every team training session? Can you avoid a trip to Aunt Karen's this week?

Set up a personal weekly planner. This is likely to change each week, so create one week at a time and fill in the study you plan to do each week. Your study time may vary depending on what hours you work, your sports or family commitments. Plus, if you are having extra tutoring you can count this towards that subject for the week. You need to ensure though that if you take extra time off, you make it up somewhere else.

We are quite aware that you will have more than just English to study for. You need to work out how many subjects you have to study and the actual commitment each subject will take. The examples we have used assume you have 5 subjects that will have up to 3 external assessments each.

ISBN 9780170244220

We have started this timetable at 9am but if you are a 'morning person' you might prefer to do an hour's study between 6.30 and 7.30 am!

> *You will find blank copies of these grids for you to create your own timetable at www.cengage.co.nz/ach-eng-yr11*

Timetable 1: For during the school week

	Mon	Tues	Wed	Thurs	Fri	Sat	Sun
9.00-10.00							Science
10.00-11.00							
11.00-12.00							English
12.00-1.00							
1.00-2.00							Maths
2.00-3.00							
3.00-4.00						English	Geo
4.00-5.00	Geo	Acc	Maths	Acc		English	
5.00-6.00							Acc
6.00-7.00	English	Maths	Science	Geo			
7.00-8.00							Science
8.00-9.00							

When school finishes you should change your timetable to reflect the increase in the time available for study. Take a look at the example below:

Timetable 2: For when school has finished

	Mon	Tues	Wed	Thurs	Fri	Sat	Sun
9-10	English	Science		Acc	English		
10.05-11.05		Acc	Maths	Geo	Science		Maths
							English
11.30-12.30	Maths	English	Geo	English	Maths		Acc
12.35-1.05	English			Maths			Science
2.00-3.00	Science	Maths	Acc		Geo	Acc	English
3.05-4.00	Acc	Geo	Science	Science	Acc	English	
							Acc
4.30-5.30	Geo		English	Science		Geo	Maths
7.00-8.00							

You will notice that there is enough space to add a sixth subject if you need to, or to add extra hours to subjects that you find more difficult. Of course you can vary your timetable to suit your life's pattern.

You need to make sure that when you are not studying that you are doing something other than sitting and watching TV! Getting some fresh air is a great way to recharge your batteries. It could be a swim, a walk (even if only to the letterbox!), a game of basketball etc.

Eat good, healthy food and drink plenty of water. Sleep is also a vital part of a good study programme – burning the midnight oil is not a useful technique for most of us.

WHAT ARE YOU GOING TO STUDY?

Your classroom teachers will provide you with some ideas for a study programme but we would like to suggest one for English revision that we know is successful.

ISBN 9780170244220

Here is a programme that will incorporate:

- 4 weeks of 4 sessions
- 2 weeks of 7 sessions (or thereabouts!)

By the time you have completed all the sessions you will be prepared for the external examinations.

Your teacher may set activities specific to your class's content, so be flexible and incorporate
his or her requirements into your programme of revision.

HOW ARE YOU PREPARING FOR STUDY?

You will also need to have sorted all your material from English classes, revision lessons, personal study, tutoring etc into a divided ring binder or separate folders.

Go through your entire room, bag, books and ask your teacher for any copies of examination essays, or marking that has not been returned to you. If you were absent for any time during the year you need to make sure you have any notes you may have missed. Your friends may be able to help, and your teacher.

You might also decide to spend some time going through the internet and/or library seeing what you can find about your text. There are often sites that give you information about your text. This information can be used to supplement your class notes and offer you some new material to refresh you memory about your text. A word of caution: Examiners are experts at seeing when a student has learnt a response off by heart. They don't appreciate this sort of revision.

Sort all your notes into a logical order. Re-writing scrappy notes tidily is a great way of reminding yourself about the topic.

It is also a VERY good idea to re-read any books or short stories or poetry or plays you have studied during the year and rewatch the film you will be using. It is amazing how much additional detail you pick up once you know a text well. Plus, by this time at the end of the year, you know what is required to write successful essays and you can find extra information to help you answer questions fully as you re-read or rewatch the text.

The sessions

Each session is designed to take you an hour of study. This does not include time to find pencils, sort paperwork, make a cup of cocoa, put out the cat etc. so you need to be organised and ready to begin actual revision.

On the following pages you will see a programme that involves you using Live-wire Learning, an online resource and a more traditional examination focus.

Live-wire LEARNING

An aside on ... Live-wire Learning

Live-wire Learning is an interactive, web-based programme that makes your revision easy, interesting, challenging and will build your confidence. With comprehensive teaching points and hundreds of questions at Achieved, Merit and Excellence levels, you can prepare yourself effectively for your English NCEA externals. The material in the teaching points will summarise and complement much of what you have learned in class. To learn as you go, click on any incorrect answers and get instant feedback from the explanation. Repeat a module a couple of times to improve your score and access more challenging questions. Check out the Results page to keep track of your successful learning.

Achievement English @ Year 11 and Live-wire Learning will put the digital edge into your education.

ISBN 9780170244220

Revision programme

BEFORE YOU BEGIN

You may have studied more than one written text this year. Before you begin you need to decide if you are going to revise all options or only the one you feel most comfortable writing about. If you are revising multiple text then make sure you evenly divide the sessions between them.

You may also find it useful to work back through this book filling in any activities you have not completed.

Note: The times allocations given in these sessions are guidelines only. You may need a few extra minutes to finish some of them, but then again we are sure there will be a few that you finish quicker so it will even out in the end!

SESSION 1

Recap your Written Text (40 minutes)
Re-read the notes notes/essays/handouts you have on your written text paying particularly attention to those on character. You may need to re-write or re-order this material as you go.

Written Text Essay - Character (20 minutes)
Now you are familiar with your notes,write a plan of how you might answer the following question:

Describe at least ONE **character or individual** you enjoyed reading about in the text(s). Explain why the character(s) or individual(s) helped you understand an idea in the text(s).

SESSION 2

Written Text Essay - Character (45 minutes)
Answer the following question using the plan you wrote in Session 1. Don't forget to quickly check over your work in case you missed something.

Describe at least ONE **character or individual** you enjoyed reading about in the text(s). Explain why the character(s) or individual(s) helped you understand an idea in the text(s).

SESSION 3

Recap of Close Reading (1 hour)
Complete the following Live-wire Learning activities:

1. Poetic Devices: Jargon
Cliché
2. Definitions: Revising Definitions in Y11 English 1
3. Close Reading of Unfamiliar Text: *Twiggy - Supermodel*

SESSION 4

Recap your Written Text (10 minutes)
Re-read any notes/handouts you have on the techniques/style of your text.

Written Text Essay (40 minutes)
Answer ONE of the following questions:

Describe at least ONE **language feature** that was used to help you understand an important idea in the text(s). Explain why that language feature(s) helped you understand a key idea(s) in the text(s).

Note: Language feature(s) could include imagery, style, vocabulary or symbolism.

OR

Describe a **memorable event** in your text(s). Explain **how** this event was made memorable for you in EACH text(s).

SESSION 5

Close Reading Recap (15 minutes)
Re-read pages 10-14 of this book.

Re-read the Written Text Language Lists on page 147 of this book.

Close Reading (45 minutes)
Complete the following Live-wire Learning activity:

Close Reading of Unfamiliar Text: *Cell Phones*

SESSION 6

Visual Text Recap (25 minutes)
Complete the following Live-wire Learning activities:

Key Features of Film 1: Editing, Style, Structure & Narration

Exemplar: Film - Saving Private Ryan

Visual Text Essay (35 minutes)
Now you have spent some time looking at how others have written essays look over your own written text notes and write a plan of how you might answer the following question:

Describe at least ONE **important conflict** in the text(s). Explain why the conflict(s) helped understand an idea in the text(s). Discuss visual/oral text features in your response.

SESSION 7

Close Reading (20 minutes)
Complete the following Live-wire Learning activity:

1. Definitions: Revising Definitions in Y11 English 2
2. Exemplar: Written text: Setting

Written Text - Setting (40 minutes)
Answer the following question:

Describe **an important aspect of setting** in the text. Explain **how** it helped you **understand a key idea** (or ideas) in the text. *Note: 'Setting' may refer to time and / or place.*

OR

If setting does not feature in your text

Describe a **surprising OR important moment or event** in the text.

Explain how visual and/or verbal features were used to help you **understand** why this moment or event was surprising OR important.

SESSION 8

Improving your work (1 hour)
Look through your year's work and find an essay (from either class work/previous examinations/study) that you have not done well.

a. Re-read the essay.
b. Re-read the comments made by your teacher.
c. Using a red pen, mark parts of the essay that you know are not done well.
d. Using a different colour pen, mark the parts of the essay you know are done well.
e. Spend 10 minutes going through your notes looking for information to improve this essay.
f. Re-write the essay.

ISBN 9780170244220

SESSION 9 **Close Reading (1 hour)** Complete the following Live-wire Learning activities: 1 Poetic Devices: Literal & Figurative Imagery Metaphor 2 Close Reading of Unfamiliar Text: Written text: *Beach Burial* (poem)	**SESSION 10** **Written Text Essay Recap (20 minutes)** Go back to the essay you wrote in Session 7. Look at it critically, and using your notes, re-work it into a successful essay. **Close Reading (40 minutes)** Complete the following Live-wire Learning activity: Close Reading of Unfamiliar Text: *Text Speak – when not to use it.*	**SESSION 11** Spend some time looking back through this book for activities that you have not completed during the year. If you have completed them all spend time learning the language lists on pages 147-152.
TAKE STOCK You are nearly halfway through your revision. Spend some time re-organising your notes/essays etc. Sort out any essays you want to take into your teacher to mark and make suggestions for improvement. Assess the timetable you have set and evaluate if it is working. You may need to make some adjustments to your life if you are struggling to find time to settle down and study. Make adjustments if necessary!	**SESSION 12** **Close Reading (1 hour)** Complete the following Live-wire Learning activities: 1 Definitions: Revising Definitions in Y11 English 3 2 Poetic Devices: Rhyme Assonance and Onomatopoeia 3 Close Reading of Unfamiliar Text: *Milking Before Dawn by Ruth Dallas*	**SESSION 13** **Close Reading (25 minutes)** Complete the following Live-wire Learning activity: 1 Definitions: Revising Definitions in Y11 English 4 2 Close Reading of Unfamiliar text: Written Text: *Ocean Temperatures Abnormal* 3 Close Reading of Unfamiliar Text: *Crossing the Canterbury Plains by Brian Turner* **Short Text Essay (35 minutes)** Describe a **change** that happened in EACH text. Explain **how** this change helped you **understand a character or individual** in EACH text.
SESSION 14 **Written Text – Theme (25 minutes)** Complete the following Live-wire Learning activity: Exemplar: Interesting ideas in The Boy in the Striped Pyjamas. **Written Text Essay - Theme (25 minutes)** Now you have spent some time looking at how others have written essays look over your own written text notes and write a plan of how you might answer the following question: Describe at least ONE **event** at or near the end of the text(s) that was important. Explain why the event helped you understand a key idea(s) in the text(s).	**SESSION 15** **Written Text Essay – Theme (45 minutes)** Answer the following question using the plan you wrote in Session 14. Don't forget to quickly check over your plan in case you missed something. Describe at least ONE **character or individual** you enjoyed reading about in the text(s). Explain why the character(s) or individual(s) helped you understand an idea in the text(s).	**SESSION 16** **Improving your work (1 hour)** Look through your year's work and find an essay (from either class work/previous examinations/study) that you have not done well. a Re-read the essay. b Re-read the comments made by your teacher. c Using a red pen, mark parts of the essay that you know are not done well. d Using a different colour pen, mark the parts of the essay you know are done well. e Spend 10 minutes going through your notes looking for information to improve this essay. f Re-write the essay.
SESSION 17 **Recap Visual text (30 minutes)** Complete the following Live-wire Learning activities: Key Features of Film 2: Costume, Lighting, Special Effects Key Features of the Film 3: Sound Features **Visual Text Essay - Theme (25 minutes)** Now you have spent some time looking at how others have written essays look over your own visual text notes and write a plan of how you might answer the following question: Describe at least ONE **character or individual** who played an important role in the text(s). Explain why the character(s) or individual(s) was important in the text(s) as a whole. Discuss visual/oral text features in your response.	**SESSION 18** **Visual Text Essay – Theme (45 minutes)** Answer the following question using the plan you wrote in Session 17. Don't forget to quickly check over your plan in case you missed something. Describe at least ONE **character or individual** who played an important role in the text(s). Explain why the character(s) or individual(s) was important in the text(s) as a whole. Discuss visual/oral text features in your response.	**SESSION 19** **Close Reading (1 hour)** Complete Live-wire Learning activities 1 Definitions: Revising Definitions in Y11 English 5 2 Close Reading Unfamiliar Text: *Slaughtering Buffalo* 3 Written Language: *Oh Crumbs*

ISBN 9780170244220

SESSION 20

Recap your Visual Text (1 hour)
Spend some time reading over the work you have done on your Visual Text. Read any class notes, handouts etc you may have. Read through essays you have written, paying particular attention to areas you could improve. Spend some time learning key quotes.

SESSION 21

Recap your Written Text (1 hour)
Spend some time reading over the work you have done on your Written Text. Read through the text you are using. Read any class notes, handouts etc you may have. Read through essays you have written, paying particular attention to areas you could improve. Spend some time learning key quotes.

SESSION 22

Recap your Visual Text (10 minutes)
Re-read the notes notes/essays/ handouts you have on your visual text paying particularly attention to those on character.

Visual Text Essay (50 minutes)
Answer the following question. Don't forget to plan!

Describe at least ONE idea that **was worth learning** about in the text(s). Explain **how** verbal and / or visual feature(s) were used to show you this idea was worth learning about.

Refer to at least ONE of the following:
Camera-work
Narrative point-of-view
Editing Structure
Colour Lighting Costumes Props

SESSION 23

Recap your Written text (1 hour)
Spend some time reading over the work you have done on your Written Text. Read any class notes, handouts etc you may have. Read through essays you have written, paying particular attention to areas you could improve. Spend some time learning key quotes.

SESSION 24

Close Reading (1 hour)
Complete the following Live-wire Learning activities:

1 Definitions: Revising Definitions in Y11 English 6
2 Language Features: Wordiness
3 Close Reading of Unfamiliar Text: Written Text – *Seal Shifting*

SESSION 25

Improving your work (1 hour)
Look through your year's work and find an essay (from either class work/previous examinations/study) that you have not done well.

a Re-read the essay.
b Re-read the comments made by your teacher.
c Using a red pen, mark parts of the essay that you know are not done well.
d Using a different colour pen, mark the parts of the essay you know are done well.
e Spend 10 minutes going through your notes looking for information to improve this essay.
f Re-write the essay.

SESSION 26

Poetic Close Reading (1 hour)
Complete the following Live-wire Learning activities:

1 Poetic Devices:
Simile
Personification
2 Close Reading of Unfamiliar Text: Written Text: *High Flight* (poem)

SESSION 27

Close Reading (1 hour)
Complete the following Live-wire Learning activities:

1 Definitions: Revising Definitions in Y11 English 7
2 Poetic devices: Clichés
3 Close Reading of Unfamiliar Text: Written Text: *Tiger Hunt* continues

SESSION 28

Visual Text (60 minutes)
Answer the following question. Don't forget to plan!
Describe **your first impression** (or impressions) of a character in the text(s). Explain **how** at least TWO of the following were **used** to **create** this impression (or impressions):

Camera work	Props
Sound effects	Costumes
Lighting	Dialogue
Narrative point of view	Special effects

SESSION 29

The Weakest Link (1 hour)
Choose the text (written or visual) that you feel is your weakest – be honest!

Spend this session going back over the work you have on this text. Re-read notes and handouts to familiarise yourself with the content again.

Now look carefully at the essays you have written on this text. Evaluate each one and look for where it could be improved.

Learn some quotes/phrases from the text that might be useful in the examination.

SESSION 30

Your last hour! Yay! Choose something you want to spend an hour 'brushing up on'. It may be something you feel you need a bit of extra time on, something you like, something you missed …

We know that you are as well prepared as possible for your Year 11 external assessments.

GOOD LUCK! See you in Year 12…

ISBN 9780170244220

My extended reading list

Remember: the more you read, the more you will understand and the better your own writing will be!

Keep your own list here of all the text that you read for your class and personal reading. Try to read a variety of text: novel, short story, magazine article, play, comic, blog poem ...

Title of Text	Author	Brief Comment

ISBN 9780170244220